THE PASSION OF BARBERING

Rico's Barber Shop Presents

THE PASSION OF BARBERING

A NEW ERA OF HAIR DESIGNERS

DR. CHARLES H. WASHINGTON

THE PASSION OF BARBERING
A NEW ERA OF HAIR DESIGNERS

iUniverse books may be ordered through booksellers or by contacting:

iUniverse
1663 Liberty Drive
Bloomington, IN 47403
www.iuniverse.com
1-800-Authors (1-800-288-4677)

Library of Congress Control Number: 2015915304

ISBN: 978-1-4917-7660-5 (sc)
ISBN: 978-1-4917-7661-2 (e)

Print information available on the last page.

iUniverse rev. date: 09/15/2015

Perspectives
from
Barbers, Clients, Owners, and Scientific Research

To my deceased parents, Nezie Lou Washington and Clee Walter Jackson.

To my lovely wife of forty-six years, life partner, and best friend, Lourdes Doble Washington, who has been patient and who has understood my desire to be successful at any and all my undertakings. No way could I have made it this far without you. I love you!

To my children, Joseph, Lillian (Blakely), Cleon, and Charletta (Wilson), all of whom I love so dearly and whom have always provided me the inspiration necessary to maintain a positive outlook on life within the community so I don't lose sight of my responsibility as a businessman to show compassion for others. After I became a daddy, you guys individually and collectively taught me how to be a father. Although I made mistakes along the way, my love for each of you never lessened.

To my grandchildren, Joseph Danté, Anthony, Jansen, Chris Jr., Kaylynn, Michael, Kendall, Caleb, Noah, and the queen Sidney Lou, all of whom I love immensely, as you give me strength to do the things necessary to establish an educational legacy for you to follow.

To all the clients of Rico's Barber Shops who imparted their wisdom, laughter, tears, and lies and who, more importantly, listened to others: this books is for and about you. Team Rico appreciates that you allowed us to provide for your hair-care needs. Please know that we take nothing for granted. We value your business and work hard to keep it, one hair service at a time.

To all the people I have touched professionally within the hair-care industry. Many of them have moved on and become entrepreneurs in their own right. I certainly hope something I said or did brought you inspiration for that journey.

To my coworkers at Rico's Barbershop & Styles, Incorporated, who have provided my family and me much love in return for providing a place to display their craftsmanship. Each member is special in a different way, bringing something special to our service menu. I salute you as kings and queens of the hair-care industry.

CHAPTERS

TABLES

FIGURES

PREFACE

This book came about as I was conducting research to support my doctoral dissertation; I quickly realized that misconceptions exist within the hair-care industry as it relates to the acceptance of diversity (race and gender) in barbershops in Riverside County, California. This writing further illustrates how barbering has transitioned rapidly away from traditional haircutting and shaving to styling and designs. Although this process is more time consuming and costly, practitioners must provide what the clientele requests. *The Passion of Barbering* clarifies some of the mistaken beliefs society has about diversity in the hair-care industry and specifically barbershops. It also demonstrates some of the pros and cons of operating an establishment in this complex industry, for both a practitioner and an owner.

This book includes information that has been tested over time and proven to be a blueprint for success in this industry and region. My intention for writing this book is to educate people interested in entering the profession by having practitioners already in the industry share their knowledge and life experiences. Competition is what makes the barbering profession better.

While writing this book, I learned that many of the hairstyles of old are returning, with younger barbers adding a more artistic form to each one. Many older barbershops are trapped in the box of just cutting hair while some are beginning to realize they are missing out on a moneymaking opportunity. According to Bozeman, almost all African American males have at least one memory of a barbershop. In past years, the barbershop was a space that found a home in virtually every community in which you found African Americans. I operate two 12-chair barbershops in the same city doing business with the fictitious business name of Rico's Barbershop & Styles, Incorporated. Both establishment's are designed and operates the same like a franchise. All 24 barbers are considered to be part of the team thereby terming them as Team Rico. Team Rico barbers also provided me with insightful information on the industry. From start to finish, it took about eighteen months to write this book. There were a couple of major setbacks due to illness, surgery, and recuperation.

I chose the title of this book to honor those who contributed to this writing and the many barbershops around the country that provide valuable services to many clients.

For a barber to become a member of Team Rico, regardless of gender, he or she must either be passionate about the industry or display a professionalism leading him or her toward becoming passionate. To learn more about Team Rico, go to www.ricoshair.com or www.ricoshair2.com. We can also be found on Instagram @Teamricosbarbershop.

ACKNOWLEDGMENTS

I can never give enough thanks to the Southern California Barbering Apprenticeship Council (SCBAC) for its genuine support of the barbering profession. Over the years, the men and women on this council have proven their unconditional commitment toward assisting personnel in overcoming obstacles to entering the barbering apprenticeship program and seeing them through to their completion—from journeymen to master barbers.

Special thanks to the former principal Charlie Brown (retired) and the vice principal Alma Angelo (retired) of the San Bernardino Adult School/ SCBAC program's lead educational advisers for their past expertise, guidance, advice, and commitment to the barbering apprenticeship program. Vice Principal Angelo's insight and contribution have enhanced an already dynamic program and have proven to be an asset to the overall operation of the SCBAC apprenticeship program.

Much appreciation to Stephanie Foster (retired) and Paul Marshall and his staff from the Department of Industrialization, Division of Apprenticeship Standards (DAS), for their insight and direction, which enable SCBAC to operate professionally within the established statewide guidelines. Mr. Marshall's workforce consistently provides a rapid response to establishment and apprentice applications submitted by the SCBAC and has contributed immensely to our effort to meet the needs of potential apprentice barbering licensees.

Thanks to Ms. Sandra Torres and Mr. Prentice Lomax of the Board of Barbering and Cosmetology for their guidance and directions with assistance in documenting correspondence and providing apprenticeship licenses in a timely and efficient manner.

Most importantly, I am grateful to the establishment owners who sacrifice their time and resources to help apprentices get to the finish line and obtain their master barber licenses. Without the aid of the shop owners, there would be no apprenticeship programs.

Just as it takes a village to raise a child, it takes many volunteers to make the program work and become successful. I salute those of you who have given many years of your time to ensure the program remained in effect. Your time served has contributed immensely to the overall success of the Southern California Barbering Apprenticeship Council.

INTRODUCTION

When I began to write this book, I was taken back to when I conducted a scientific survey to support the hypothesis of my dissertation. Surveys were conducted with both clients and barbershop owners to find out their thoughts about having a diverse workforce as it relates to race and gender. Surprisingly, they were on the opposite ends of the spectrum. The vast percentage of establishment owners preferred no diversity in their clientele and was adamantly against having females on their staff. However, clients preferred diversity in the barbering staff and enjoyed mingling with people of other ethnicities or backgrounds.

After twenty years in the hair-care industry, I have found little reason not to side with the clients. I find the opinions of establishment owners to be shortsighted, bad for business, and based on shallow, uninformed thinking. Perhaps in past years this mind-set could have been supportable when operating a single-chair barbershop serving a specific neighborhood. However, the opinions expressed in this book validate diversity in all areas of the hair-care industry.

The perception is that African American barbers do not have the expertise to cut or service straight hair and that barbers of Caucasian descent lack the knowledge necessary to cut African American hair.

My dissertation's title is "Do Significant Differences Exist in the Racial and Gender Makeup in Barbershops in Riverside County, California," and it involved two questions:

1. Why are barbershops in Riverside County, California, not diverse in regard to race and gender?
2. How does the Riverside County hair-care industry support racial and gender diversity?

Two hypotheses were tested:

1. There is no significant difference in the racial and gender makeup of barbers in Riverside County, California.
2. The Riverside County hair-care industry supports race and gender diversity.

In an effort to establish answers to those research questions, I distributed a twenty-question survey among various barbershops and beauty salons within fifteen of the most populated cities in Riverside County, California. The cities were chosen because of their population density and the prospect of gathering sufficient data to resolve the hypotheses. All questions asked of owners, shop managers, or leading practitioners contributed both directly and indirectly to reaching a conclusion. All data collected were sorted and categorized separately by city.

This process allowed me to determine how each city's data contributed to the overall outcome. Of the 250 distributed questionnaires, 199 were returned completed with sufficient data to be used for the research. The median number of owners responding was 144. The highest number was 199, and the lowest number was 89. However, some respondents declined to answer some of the questions. The questionnaires returned blank could not be used in any of the equations. The statistical data resulted only from answers provided by the respondents. The tables in this book contain only a few of the questions asked of those surveyed.

Questionnaire Results

- The questionnaire asked owners to provide the number of barbers working in their establishments. The variables provided were (a) one to three or (b) four or more. Of the questionnaires returned, 114 businesses that they operate with one to three barbers, and 66 often said they employed four or more barbers. Table 1 shows the percentages.

- The next question asked how many of the barbers on staff were women. The variables provided were (a) one to three, (b) four or more, and (c) none. The questionnaire revealed that 83 owners employed one to three females, 31 owners listed four or more, and 55 owners reported they had no females on their staff. Table 2 shows the statistical makeup.
- Owners were asked to list the various ethnicities in their barber workforce. Owners were provided the following categories: African American, Asian American, American Indian, Caucasian, Hispanic, and Others. There were 193 respondents. Table 3 contains the breakdown of barbers by ethnicity and the percentages.
- Another important factor that contributed to the study's conclusion was the average age of the barbers. The variables provided to the 181 respondents were (a) eighteen to twenty-five, and (b) twenty-six and above. The percentages of the average ages of barbers are in table 4.
- An additional factor required for evaluation was the geographic location of the participants' establishment. Variable options provided were (a) a mall or (b) a neighborhood. See table 5 for the breakdown.
- Since barbers entering this industry have to build a clientele base to be successful, establishment owners were asked to provide the number of personnel working full or part time. The variables provided were (a) one to three, (b) four or more, and (c) all of them. Table 6 contains the percentages as reported by 181 respondents.
- The longevity of a business often represents success. Therefore, it was important to determine how long an establishment had been operational. The variables were (a) one to three years, (b)

four to ten years, and (c) eleven years or more. See table 7 for the percentages of business operation among 175 respondents.

- Barbers often consider themselves to be self-employed. Therefore, the owners provided the type of work relationship they had with the barbers in their establishment. The variables provided were (a) booth rental, (b) independent contractor, (c) percentage basis, and (d) a combination of any of them. The work conditions percentages for the 169 respondents are found in table 8.
- An additional aspect presented on the questionnaire was the work methods of the barbers as it related to providing service to clients. Owners were asked how their barbers work. The variables provided were (a) appointments, (b) walk-ins, or (c) a combination of both. Table 9 lists the results by percentages of the 182 respondents. Owners were asked to describe the waiting times for clients to be served. The variables provided were (a) one to ten minutes, (b) eleven to twenty minutes, or (c) twenty-one minutes or longer. Table 10 shows the percentages for the 199 respondents.
- For an establishment within the hair-care industry to embrace diversity fully, the practitioners must be capable of servicing hair of all textures. Participants were asked to indicate either variable (a) yes or (b) no regarding their barbers' skills in servicing all textures of hair. Percentages of the 89 respondents are contained in table 11.
- Business owners were asked about their establishment's position as to representing diversity of race and gender. The question asked was "Do you believe your customer base would improve if your establishment was diverse with race and gender?" The variables utilized were (a) yes or (b) no. The 180 respondents' percentages can be viewed in table 12.
- Finally, the owners were asked, if the opportunity presented itself, would they consider diversifying their staff by hiring someone of a different race and gender? Variables presented

were (a) yes or (b) no. The response of 182 respondents can be viewed at table 13.

In addition, I conducted a twelve-question survey. The case-study research provided a self-administered survey to potential hair-care clients ages eighteen and older; it contained multiple-choice questions based on a five-level Likert scale. This scale numerically rated the answers on a scale of one to five, with one being highly unlikely and five being very likely. The questions were designed to determine how receptive clients would be to the diversification of the hair-care practitioners in an establishment and to provide a process to test the significance of the stated hypotheses.

Of the 350 surveys taken, 341 were completed with sufficient data for the research. The median number of survey responses was 221. The largest number of responses was 341, and the lowest was 101. However, for various reasons, some respondents declined to answer some or all the questions. The statistical data results only from the answers provided by respondents with adequate data for proper usage.

1. The initial question asked was "Would you allow a female practitioner to service your hair?" Table 14 shows the percentages for the following ratings: (a) "Strongly agree" netted 118 of the population, followed by (b) "Agree" with 120 of the total count, and then (c) "Neither agree nor disagree" with 42 of the population. Finally, (d) and (e) "Disagree" or "Strongly disagree" were combined with 25 of the total count.
2. Participants were asked if they would let someone of a different race service their hair. An astounding 307 respondents answered with (a) and (b) "Strongly agree" and "Agree" while 11 percent reported that it (c) did not matter, and 12 percent flat-out noted (d) and (e) disagreement. See table 15.
3. Gender plays an important role in the selection of a practitioner. Therefore, participants were asked if they would patronize an establishment in which all the barbers were female. Of the

311 respondents, 45 percent noted their (a) and (b) agreement, 22 percent seemed unconcerned, and (c) neither agreed nor disagreed, and the remaining 33 percent adamantly against female barbers (d) and (e) disagreed with the proposal of an all-female barbershop. See table 16.

4. Segregation is very common within the hair-care industry of Riverside County; therefore, I posed a question to participants regarding whether they would patronize a barbershop that services people of various ethnicities. Table 17 displays how the 341 respondents replied to this question. A combined 60 percent (a) agreed, and of that group, 24 percent (b) strongly 63 agreed. An indifferent group of 14 percent (c) neither agreed nor disagreed and an even split of 26 percent either (d) and (e) disagreed or strongly disagreed.
5. In an effort to explore diversity, participants were asked if they would receive hair services at a barbershop that supports diversity with barbers as it relates to race and gender. Of the 312 respondents 65 that replied, 71 percent (a) and (b) agreed with the diversity proposal while 16 percent showed (c) indifference and 13 percent (d) and (e) disagreed. See table 18.
6. To adequately measure the maturity of the respondents, it was important to establish an age category. Table 19 illustrates that (a) the age group of 18 to 20 represented 19 percent of the replies, (b) the age group of 21 to 25 represented 24 percent, (c) the age group of 26 to 30 represented 13 percent, and (d) the age group of 31 and above represented 44 percent. There were a total of 267 respondents. This question was statistically immeasurable, however; I sought them only to obtain the age category of the participants.
7. Respondents were asked to note their ethnicity. Table 20 provides a chart that demonstrates 9 percent of participants noted (a) Caucasian decent; 37 percent registered (b) Hispanic; 42 percent indicated (c) African American; 4 percent listed (d) Asian American or American Indian; and the remaining 8 percent recorded (e) an ethnicity other than one previously

listed. This was immeasurable, but I only sought to obtain the ethnicities of the participants for information purposes.

In order to improve customer service in a professional manner, within a hair care establishment, first and foremost, the entire staff must buy into the process and have a desire towards providing the services to clients in an expeditious manner. As an establishment owner, I encourage the entire barber staff to greet entering clients and make eye contact with them. Verbal communication in conjunction with eye contact provides the clients a feeling warmth and welcome.

After retiring from the Marine Corps and while residing in Oceanside, California, I approached a so-called brother with a barbering establishment, wanting to pick his brains about getting started in the industry. He refused to talk to me either in person or on the telephone. I tried to make an appointment to get my hair cut (this was back when I had hair), and he refused to cut my hair for fear that I would corner him into communicating about how to get established in the industry. Over the years, I found many African American barbershop owners to be selfish and backstabbing, with the old crab-in-the-bucket mentality. Not wanting to share their knowledge and experiences for fear of competition. During my journey in the industry, I made a few mistakes on the business side, and I learned from those costly experiences. Being selfish was surely not a mistake I made. I can attest to assisting more than twenty-five young men on how to get their business started. Many of which I mentored along the way until they were ready for that entrepreneur step.

Two Caucasian barbershop owners took time from their busy schedules to share with me the inner workings that made them successful. They warned me that what worked for them may not work for me, because my target audience was different from theirs. How wrong they were! I never let them know that I had a specific target audience I would market toward; I knew from the onset that I would seek a diverse staff that would produce a diverse clientele base.

After I opened my business, the owner that had refused to give me guidance was seen on several occasions by myself and other barbers viewing my business from a distance (Tri City Square Barbershop) with binoculars, undoubtedly seeing his former customers entering. Our businesses were ten miles apart; however, my shop was in a prime location with a nationally known eatery.

The return on investment (ROI) for my startup was earned in less than two years. So I made it a point that I would always share my ideas and views to help others become entrepreneurs in the industry. I also decided to go back to college and get a degree in business. As of this writing, I have three degrees under the business umbrella and provide consulting in various areas of business.

When I relocated to Southwest Riverside County, I intended to retire from the industry. However, a former employee that I had mentored requested that I help him at his shop a few days a week. I agreed, but after a few weeks of working, I noticed how unprofessional he was to both employees and clients alike. One of the younger barbers approached and asked me to be his partner in opening a business. My former employee found out and, in the middle of a haircut, told me to leave his shop.

I had established a sizable clientele base of older men, so I operated from a beauty salon until our shop became operational. I had seized the opportunity. At that time there were only two locations where African American men could get service for their hair. This was during a housing boom, and all the surrounding cities were growing faster than their ability to provide enough infrastructures to support the communities.

The partnership business opened, and once again our competitors were using binoculars. After a couple of years, the partnership was dissolved because of differences of opinion on how to operate the business as well as misappropriation of the business's finances. So, during my consultations, I advise anyone not to go into a partnership, because there are too many negatives.

Many in the industry say that the difference between a good haircut and a bad one is two weeks (because the hair grows back). From my experience in the industry, the biggest factor in client retention is not how well the barber cuts hair, but rather if a relationship is formed. Most clients return because of the experience.

In some multichair barbershops, the most talented barbers are the least requested, while less talented barbers are booked. The booked barbers seem to be those with the most compelling personalities.

Albert Einstein once said that insanity is to continue to do the same thing over and over again and expect a different result. If a barber expects to build his or her clientele base and make more money, continuing to do the same thing is insane.

Many barbers make the mistake of moving from shop to shop, hoping to make more money, when the key is to improve the level of service they provide in the shop they currently work in. A truly good barber can succeed almost anywhere by creating the ideal experience for clients and adhering to the principles, examples, and philosophies presented in the upcoming chapters.

The $20 billion US hair-care industry is overwhelmingly focused on women, according to Green (2014). Of the eighty-six-thousand brick-and-mortar establishments, eighty-two thousand are beauty salons. Green projected a growth of the industry worldwide in 2014 as high as 8.5 percent. Part of that growth curve in the United States can be attributed to the rise in sales of men's grooming products and the success of the four thousand barbershops catering to men and families.

There is no place like an African American barbershop; you get to find out what is really on the minds of people. No subjects are off the table when it comes to barbershop talk. Everyone can listen, comment, be silent, or laugh.

CHAPTER ONE

MODERN BARBERS AND BARBERING

The Origin of *Barber*

According to *Milady's Standard Professional Barbering* by Maura Scali-Sheahan (2011), the word *barber* is derived from the Latin word *barba*, meaning "beard." Another Latin word, *tonsorial*, means the cutting, clipping, or trimming of hair with shears or a razor.

The Egyptian culture is credited with being the first to develop beauty in an extravagant fashion. Excavations from tombs have revealed such historical objects as combs, brushes, mirrors, cosmetics, scissors, and razors made of tempered copper and bronze.

Scali-Sheahan asserts that the golden age of barbershops was from the 1880s through the 1940s. Barbers became organized and started the Barbers Protection Association in 1886. The following year, the association became affiliated with the American Federation of Labor. There were two categories of barber: the master barber group and journeyman barber group, says Scali-Sheahan.

In Africa, hair was groomed with complicated carved combs and decorated with beads, clay, and colored bands. Braiding of the hair was widespread, with complex patterns denoting the individual's status within his or her tribe, says Scali-Sheahan.

Greek-Sicilian barbers introduced shears to Rome in 700 to 800 BC. During Greece's Golden Age (500–300 BC), barbering became a highly developed art. Barbershops became the gathering places for sporting, social, and political news. As such, barbers rose in importance and status to become leading citizens within their social structure. Barbers were virtually unknown in Rome until 296 BC, says Scali-Sheahan.

Barber-Surgeons

According to Scali-Sheahan, by the Middle Ages, barbers not only provided tonsorial services but also entered the world of medicine by taking over the phlebotomy services once provided by priest and clergy, which was forbidden by Alexander III. Barbers continued the practice of bloodletting, minor surgery, herbal remedies, and tooth pulling for centuries. They were referred to as barber-surgeons and formed their first organization in France in AD 1096. By the 1100s, a guild of surgeons specialized in the study of medicine.

The Worshipful Company of Barbers guild was formed in London in 1308 with the objective of regulating and overseeing the profession. There were two classes of barbers: one performed hair-care services, and the other specialized in surgeries. By 1368, surgeons had formed their own guild with oversight by the Barber's Guild; it lasted until 1462, according to Scali-Sheahan. In 1540, Henry VIII reunited the barbers and surgeons of London by granting a charter to the Company of Barber Surgeons. However, with the advancement of medicine, the practice of bloodletting became obsolete. Although the barber-surgeons' medical practice had dwindled, they were still relied on to dispense medicinal herbs and pull teeth.

The first barber-surgeons' corporation was formed in France in 1094. French barber-surgeons under the rule of the king's barber formed a guild in 1371 that lasted until about the time of the French Revolution.

During the nineteenth century, wigs became so complicated and fashionable that a separate corporation of barber-wigmakers was founded in France. Not until 1779 was a corporation formed in Prussia; it was disbanded in 1809, when new unions were started.

Scali-Sheahan noted that many Europeans had become so dependent on the services of the barber-surgeons that Dutch and Swedish settlers brought barber-surgeons with them to America to ensure the well-being of the immigrants.

Customs and Traditions

According to Scali-Sheahan, as barbering became widespread, so did its customs and traditions. In almost every early culture, hairstyles have indicated social status. Some of the traditions are as follows:

- Noblemen of ancient Gaul indicated their rank by wearing their hair long. This continued until Caesar made them cut it when he conquered them, as a sign of submission.
- In ancient Greece, boys cut their hair when they reached adolescence.
- Hindu boys would shave their heads upon reaching adolescence.
- Following the invasion of China by Manchu, Chinese men adopted the line as a mark of dignity and manhood, in modern time the line is referred to as a part in the hair.
- Ancient Britons were extremely proud of their long, blond hair.
- The Danes, Angles, and Normans dressed their hair for beautification, adornment, and ornamentation before battles with the Britons.
- In ancient Rome, the color of a woman's hair indicated her class or rank. Noblewomen tinted their hair red; middle class women colored their hair blonde; and poor women were compelled to color their hair black.

- At various times in Roman history, slaves would be allowed or not allowed to wear beards, depending on the dictates of the ruler at the time.
- In later centuries, a person's religion, occupation, and politics influenced the length and styles of hair and the wearing of beards.
- Clergymen of the Middle Ages were distinguished by a shaved patch on the top of their head, called tonsuring. In 1972, the Roman Catholic Church abolished the practice of tonsure.

The First Barber School

In 1893, A. B. Moler established America's first barber school in Chicago, according to Scali-Sheahan. In that same year, he published the first barbering textbook, *The Moler Manual of Barbering*. In 1897, Minnesota became the first state to pass a barber-licensing law; it established standards for sanitation, minimum education for barbers, and licensing requirements for both barbers and barbershops. This legislation set the standards for sterilizing, sanitizing, and replacing barbering equipment.

Barbershops were considered hangouts where men gathered to socialize; they often rivaled saloons and cafés. Men frequently stopped by their favorite barbershops not only for a haircut or shave but also to hang out, play dominoes with friends, and chew the fat. These places were classy, with stunning marble counters lined with colorful blown-glass tonic bottles. The barber chairs were elaborately carved from oak and walnut, and fitted with fine leather upholstery.

From 1960 to 1970 as cosmetologists entered this predominantly male industry, manufacturers decreased the masculinity of barber chairs, making them much lighter, removing the reclining capability, and decreasing the size of the back bars.

The Barber Pole

According to Scali-Sheahan, a barber pole is thought to represent the staff that a patient would hold tightly so the veins in his arm would stand out during bloodletting. The bottom end cap of the modern barber pole represents the basin used either to catch the blood during bloodletting or to lather the face during shaving. The white stripes on the poles represent the bandages used to stop the bleeding, which were then hung on the staff to dry. The stained bandages would twist around the pole in the breeze, forming a red-and-white pattern. One interpretation of the colors of the barber pole is that the red represented the blood, the blue represented veins, and white represented bandages.

When the Barber-Surgeon Company was formed in England, barbers were required to use blue-and-white poles and surgeons red-and-white poles. It is also thought that the red, white, and blue poles displayed in the United States originated in deference to the nation's flag. Modern barbers have retained the barber pole as the primary symbol of the profession of barbering. It is prohibited in some states to display a barber pole at any establishment that is not a licensed barbershop employing licensed barbers, according to Scali-Sheahan.

CHAPTER TWO

REGULATING THE HAIR-CARE INDUSTRY

With the exception of some counties in Alabama, all states have laws regulating the practice of barbering and hairstyling. Regulation commenced in 1929. The Department of Consumer Affairs and the Board of Barbering and Cosmetology are the governing bodies responsible for regulating the hair-care industry in California. These governing bodies are responsible for testing and licensing master barbers, cosmetologists, and barber apprentices. The Board of Barbering also regulates the licensing of hair-care establishments. The board's primary responsibility is to protect the health, safety, and welfare of the public as it relates to hair care (California Barbering, 2013).

In addition is the National Barber Board, which has the following objectives:

- to promote the exchange of information between state barber boards and state agencies examining, licensing, and regulating the barber industry
- to develop standards and procedures for examining barbers
- to develop standards for licensing and policing the barber industry
- to develop a curriculum for educating barbers
- to promote continuing education in the barber industry

- to develop and promote procedures for ensuring that the consumer is informed and protected.

In concert with the Board of Barbering and Cosmetology, the Department of Industrial Relations' Division of Apprenticeship Standards is responsible for regulating the wages and training of barber apprentices. Barber students attending an accredited, full-time school are under the direct control of and are monitored by the Board of Barbering and Cosmetology.

In California, apprenticeship is a system in which barbers learn while they earn, and they learn by doing. Apprenticeship combines training with on-the-job work and supplemental instruction at a school (California Department of Industrial Relations, n.d.). The barber program operates under apprenticeship training standards agreed to by both labor and management in accordance with state and federal laws. This process allows a person to work with a master barber and gain on-the-job experience and knowhow. An apprentice barber becomes an integral part of the barbering occupation.

In this industry in which management and some labor organizations exist, each selects an agreeable number of members to serve on the joint apprenticeship committee. The committee determines the standards for training and supervises the training.

To be successful, the apprentice must have perseverance, ambition, and initiative. An apprenticeship is not unlike getting a college education; the successful completion of an apprenticeship term does not come easily, but is the result of hard work. The ability to do advanced arithmetic and to read, write, and speak well is beneficial in any walk of life, but in barbering, it is even more important. Barber apprentice must have the ability to work with others, be personable, and have a neat appearance, since contact with the public is involved. People with a high school diploma or its equivalent are preferred. The Joint Apprenticeship Committee (JAC) must supervise all barber apprenticeship training.

However, in some areas of the country they are referred to as a Joint Apprenticeship and Training Committee (JATC), or a Unilateral Apprenticeship Committee (UAC).

The training is spelled out in apprenticeship standards developed by local apprenticeship committees with the assistance of consultants from the Division of Apprenticeship Standards and is registered with the state. The processes of the trade and the number of hours to be spent learning each process are defined. The period of training is two years (California Department of Industrial Relations, n.d.).

Barber apprentices receive minimum wage for the first year and an increase of one dollar in the final year of the program. Apprentices are required to attend technical classes that supplement the training on the job, giving them a comprehensive understanding of the theoretical aspects of their work. Related instruction is one of the fundamental features of apprenticeship and has been developed and accepted as standard practice in the hair-care industry.

In most cases, this means attending classes for four hours on selected days, totaling at least 108 hours annually. In class, apprentices learn the theories of barbering; on the job they learn its practice under the supervision of a master barber. Instruction in haircutting and hair maintenance is provided to apprentices early in their training. Barber apprentices are required to furnish their own hand tools, and grants are available (California Department of Industrial Relations, n.d.).

Each apprentice is required to sign an apprentice agreement with a JAC, UAC, or an individual employer. This agreement is filed with the Division of Apprenticeship Standards. Upon successful completion of training, the barber is issued a certificate of completion by the State of California. Coordinators of apprenticeships and field representatives are employed by these boards to supervise the training of apprentices, to process apprentice applications, to keep records of progress, and the like. Barbering coordinators and apprenticeship consultants of the

Division of Apprenticeship Standards visit establishments to determine the on-the-job progress of apprentices, to seek new apprentices, and to discuss problems with apprentices, supervisors, or employers (California Department of Industrial Relations, n.d.).

The State of California's role, through the Division of Apprenticeship Standards, is consultative and developmental. The division's field and technical staff assist management, labor, JACs, and UACs by promoting and developing training programs, by providing technical data through research on current trends and training practices to improve and enlarge existing programs, and by serving as the registration and certification agency for apprenticeship in California.

The Division carries out the regulations formulated by the California Apprenticeship Council, which is charged by law to "foster, promote, and develop the welfare of the apprentice and industry, improve the working conditions of apprentices, and advance their opportunities for profitable employment." Additional guidelines are for these programs are noted in the Shelly-Maloney Apprentice Labor Standards Act of 1939.

The council's regulations are spelled out in title 8, chapter 2 of the California Administrative Code. Of particular interest are the sections pertaining to nondiscrimination (California, Department of Industrial Relations, n.d.). Apprenticeship programs must comply with the State of California Plan for Equal Opportunity.

The Division's State Plan, developed to meet the requirements of revised 29 CFR 30, is spelled out in the booklet "State of California Plan for Equal Opportunity in Apprenticeship," which also contains administrative guidelines for implementing the plan. The National Barber Board routinely proposes changes.

Some of the changes that improved the practice of barbering during the twentieth century include the following:

- the implementation of regulatory and educational standards for the program
- improved cleaning practices in the barbershop
- the availability and use of better implements and tools
- the availability and use of electrical appliances in shops
- the study of anatomy, dealing with those parts of the head, face, and neck serviced by the barber
- the study of products and preparations used in facial, scalp, and hair treatments

CHAPTER THREE

TRANSITION OF BARBERSHOP LOCATIONS

Many who have been in the hair-care industry for a long time recognize a rapid decline in traditional neighborhood barbershops. Some suggest the cause is the increasing number of national chain hair-care establishments operating in close proximity to neighborhoods, in traditional malls or strip malls that target shoppers of all kinds.

To remain competitive enough to hold off some of the chain-operated competition, neighborhood shops relocated out of the neighborhoods themselves to main thoroughfares in mini-malls and much closer to mainstream America.

When barbershops left the neighborhoods, community leadership was also lost. Neighborhood barbershops had been social gathering places for playing dominoes or catching up on the latest gossip. In barbershops, boys were taught how to become men. No matter the location of the new sites popping up, they gradually minimized the role of barbers as leaders in their communities. (This will be discussed further in chapter 11.)

Many contend that barbershops relocated to compete with franchise hair care establishments having minimal consideration of the neighborhoods that provided them business over the years. I have seen this first-hand;

parents would have their kids stop on the way home from school to get a haircut, as many stay-at-home mothers had no automobile. In an effort to maintain economic stability, barbershop owners unknowingly created problems for their clients and even themselves. Relocating does not guarantee there will be success in gaining a new clientele base.

A great percentage of the practitioners in the chain-operated shops were women, and those working in traditional barbershops were men. However, there has been a gradual transition to men working as cosmetologist and women transitioning into the craft and art of cutting and styling men's hair. Barbershops were a male-dominated environment until the turn of the early nineties. My employees claim the ratio of women to men is two to one at hair shows, which draw five hundred to 1,500 hair-care professionals.

CHAPTER FOUR

CLIENT AND WORKFORCE DIVERSITY

Many barbershops and hair salons, both privately owned and chain, cater to one type of client when it comes to race and gender, so their workforces are basically homogeneous. However, as a career military person, I was introduced to workforce diversity early on in life, and I believe that if it can work for the military, it can work in a multi-chair barbershop. Diversity in both the workforce and the clientele base has proven to be a win-win situation.

I chose to build a business diverse in both race and gender. In November 1994, my first establishment had six stations. The workforce consisted of one female and four male. The racial breakdown was one Caucasian, four African American, and one Filipino. I did this to cultivate a diverse clientele base that would generate and increase various sources of revenue.

As a result of the shop's popularity, the Caucasian and Filipino decided to stop working with me open their individual shops in a different city, as a result of their departure the diversity of my workforce dwindled. Yet I was able to maintain a diverse clientele by hiring an African American female.

I stress to my barbers that if they provide a high-quality product, treat their clients with respect, and stay away from politics and religion, and they will be successful in the hair-care industry. Again, the survey conducted during my dissertation process revealed that 95 percent of the shop owners surveyed did not support a diverse workforce staff, even if the clientele base was diverse. Tables 4.1 through 4.20 pertain.

There can be unforeseen problems related to gender diversity. However, contingent upon the number of employees, structure, management, ownership, and especially the organization's culture, most of those problems can be minimized.

Many factors keep a client returning to the same barber.

- Consistency: Providing the same nice haircut every time.
- Professionalism: How a client is greeted and treated while in the confines of the establishment. Men just getting off from a long days work tend to sit with their mouths closed and only desire a conversation when the barber has finished servicing them.
- Wait time: Many clients prefer having an appointment because it allows them to plan their day without waiting to be serviced.
- Camaraderie: Some clients could care less about the hair-care service itself because of the friendship established between the barber and client.
- Price: I believe that price has never been a determining factor for middle-aged men. However, senior citizens don't even like to pay the special senior price.

Often, when a client has a bad experience, he tends to place a bad label on the shop and, more importantly, on the barber. It is important for multiple barbers in one shop to work as a team because actions or inactions are a direct reflection on all of them. On the other side of the spectrum, contingent on the perks being offered, some clients return regardless of the perfection or professionalism presented during the service. Many clients believe in a giving barbers a second opportunity to get it right. However, a good barber does what is necessary to stay out of that category.

My research showed that some men, mostly elderly, want women only to cut their hair because of the pampering and soft touch of a woman. This category of men prefers the chain establishments because they have practitioner trainees with long fingernails to give them relaxing head massages and shampoos.

Recently, media have become major factors as the younger generations select a barber or barbershop. In January 2015, a radio station began catering mainly to barbers and barbershops. Instagram seems to be the most popular social media site for barbers because clients can view a barber's work prior to committing to his service.

In a survey, a few dozen men were asked how they choose their barbers and stylists. The following were revealed:

- Sixty-three percent noted that they stayed with the same barber, but for many different reasons. The top reasons included quality, consistency, and haircut price.
- Forty-five percent said price was a factor and that they would pay more than fifteen dollars for a haircut, and some would also include a tip.
- Fifty-one percent said that the quality of a haircut is the most important factor when choosing a permanent barber.

CHAPTER FIVE

ARTISTIC STYLING

At the turn of the twentieth century, men's hairstyles involved chemicals, braids, crew cuts, pompadours, flat tops, afros, and the like. Women started wearing short hair and getting haircuts at what were once traditional men's barbershops. More recently, young barbers have become innovative and artistic, cutting letters and designs into hair. These young artists also began challenging their abilities by attending and competing in hair shows, which is recognized as continuing education within the industry. Most barber schools and barber apprenticeship programs recognize and reward student for attending these events.

Nick the Barber shared this with me:

> This new generation of barbers are bringing back the old styles but adding a big twist to them. Many of these young practitioners have a natural gift for creating their own styles in the form of letterings or pictures. For example, one may not know how to draw but can cut designs into someone's head. These trends change fast; they come and go within a couple of months. Often by the time someone learns the new trend a new one has surfaced. (Personal interview, June 23, 2014)

While Andis, Wahl, and Oster are the major professional clipper manufacturers, barbers are customizing clippers to meet their needs. "It would be impossible to accomplish some of the designs with the traditional clippers," says Nick. "Social media can be credited for the success of barbering or hair show competition. The most popular social media for barbers displaying their talent is Instagram because of it immediacy, followed by YouTube, Facebook, and Twitter."

Nick started his career with Rico's Barber Shop and Styles, Inc., as an apprentice under my tutelage. Since then, he has become one of the premiere hair-care practitioners in Southern California. Nick explains that he got there by being hungry for more than learning how to do a traditional haircut as well as by being unselfish with techniques he learned from others. He says there are three major hair show events for barbers: Xotic Hair Battle Tour, which travels throughout the United States; International Barber and Hair Expo, an annual show in Long Beach, California; and the granddaddy of them all, the Barber Expo, held annually in Connecticut. Nick is one of the judges for the Xotic Hair Battle Tour, where each competition has five winners in various categories, including cash, trophies, medals, gift cards, and clippers.

When asked about attending hair competitions, barber Ken Diaz said, "I do not want to be painted into a box as a practitioner only capable of cutting the traditional styles" (personal interview, June 23, 2014). He has a desire to enhance his career through more education and increasing his earning through sales of products as well as branding his merchandise. He believes that young barbers who fail to take advantage of educational opportunities and learn the latest styles and techniques will be left behind or find themselves going into another vocation.

Ken would like to be able to work with barber schools, demonstrating the techniques required for cutting the many different styles clients may request. He also says it is important for barbers not to become complacent with the status quo and to place more emphasis on cutting children's hair in order to acquire more longtime clients.

Ken is a proponent of using Instagram for displaying talent, allowing barbers who do styles and designs to net profits substantially above those of barbers doing regular haircuts. (See samples of Ken's work in figures 5.1 and 5.2 below.) A regular haircut in Riverside County ranges from five dollars on the low end to twenty-five (without designs), depending on the local market.

Many barbers leave the trade after a few years, largely because of the unfavorable working conditions (low wages, evening and weekend work, as well as heavy competition from shops in close proximity). There are always opportunities in the hair-care industry as a result of attrition through retirement and, to a lesser degree, because of an increase in employment opportunities.

CHAPTER SIX

BARBERSHOP ENTERTAINMENT

When I was a young man growing up in the South in the sixties, the music being played was soft jazz, blues, or Gospel. When I opened my first barbershop, only music pleasing to the ears of the clients would be played during operating hours. Televisions were to play news, sports, or kids' programs when appropriate. Barbers were instructed that the entertainment was for the customers, not the barbers.

Until the new millennium, music was played either on a stereo or a tape player. Since the advent of the Internet, we can connect with music stations around the world and can download music, and Generation Y barbers have taken full advantage of this.

Practitioners now choose the entertainment in barbershops. Most play loud, boisterous rap music with lyrics that seasoned clients can't understand.

Barber Jonathan Baker says the music makes the day go by faster. (See a sample of Jonathan's styling abilities in figure 6.1. below).

It gets and keeps the barbers in a groove while cutting hair (personal communication, June 23, 2014). He's an avid South Eastern Conference (SEC) football fan himself, specifically Alabama and Auburn. Having multiple televisions located strategically throughout the establishment enables all customers to view what is being aired. Jonathan concludes that customers of all age and gender enjoy watching sports while waiting to be services. The shop's Wi-Fi password is posted on the bulletin board, so both the barbers and their clients have use of it.

Jonathan said the barbers provide entertainment too. Most barbers like to tell jokes to make the time go by faster. Sometimes women bring their sons to get a haircut and get to experience firsthand the humor that goes on in a barbershop. Sometime barbers have a bad day at work, just like everyone else, and they send someone out with a bad cut; that could be the joke of the day. Or someone comes in wearing outdated clothes, thinking they are clean and cool. For this reason, barbershop entertainment should never be taken personally or seriously.

CHAPTER SEVEN

PROFESSIONAL IMAGE

My hair-care establishment has a strict but legitimate workforce dress code that meets a standard agreeable to both genders. However, it's apparent that surrounding establishments have no dress code in force. Their barbers wander around with short trousers and/or sandals, both of which are a safety hazard. This type of shop doesn't have air-conditioning and targets a Generation X clientele.

It is just as important for barbers to keep both their head and their facial hair looking healthy and clean. Consistency is one of the main reasons a client keeps going back to the same barber, so the barber should always be groomed in a consistent manner. A barber's own hairstyle doesn't have to change with the times, but should be neatly tapered. Barbers sell haircuts and overall appearance makeovers; therefore, their appearance can make the difference between gaining and keeping a new client.

Most customer notice when you take pride in your appearance. A barber's clothes should be clean, freshly ironed and stain-free. Even if you have a uniform or mandatory dress code, you have some control over how you look. Your clothes should fit properly—not too tight, baggy, or sagging with undergarments showing.

Female barbers should refrain from wearing a dress or blouse with spaghetti straps. Females, if you have the freedom to wear whatever you want, please be cautious and not send the wrong signal. You are in the barber profession, and you should make sure you look like a professional. The more professional you look, the more your clients will have confidence in your ability. You will also be able to charge more than if you wear short pants and flip-flops, as if you are going to the gym.

Select shoes that are comfortable. You are going to be standing up all day, so don't wear shoes with elevated heels. Stay away from open-toed shoes or sandals as well, which are against sanitary codes and increase the risk of getting a hair sliver and an infection. Find a balance between looks and comfort, and always keep your style professional.

When wearing jewelry, stay away from big, dangling necklaces, which can be distracting and can dangle in the customer's face. Dangling jewelry can also catch on your cutting tools, combs, or other instruments. Regarding a watch: be sure yours is not too expensive, because you are going to get it wet and get product on it.

As people say in the business world, "Dress for success." Barbers should dress like the clients they desire to serve. If you always maintain a professional image, you will attract customers who also take pride in the way they look. These are the customers that do not mind paying good money for your services, tip well, and appreciate your professionalism.

There is a certain way a client should talk to a barber or stylist. Alexander (n.d.) asserts that your hair is a critical part of your total package; it influences how people feel about you.

Chaperones of boys sometimes suggest to the barber a haircut that is not fitting for the boy's face and head. It falls back on the barber to educate the chaperones about a haircut that will complement the boy's facial features and enhance his looks. This can all be accomplished through effective two-way communication.

What if your barber is on vacation and you need a haircut? Your two alternatives are to find someone else to service your needs or to wait until your barber returns. That's why it is good for clients to observe the other barbers in the shop.

Most barbers who relocate within the same geographical area as their former shop contact their clients to make them aware of the change. Some clients will follow them, while others will not. That is the nature of the business. Clients do not like barbers that move around frequently; they are reluctant to become attached, not knowing when the next move will be.

Barbers and clients sometimes don't realize that haircutting terminology isn't consistent from barber to barber and from coast to coast. Most barbershops have pictures of styles on the walls. However, the style you prefer may not be exactly depicted by one of those pictures. If you bring your own picture, the barber will know exactly what you are looking for.

California barber schools and barber apprenticeship programs train their students in the process of knowing what hairstyle will work with a hair type, head shape, and face shape. If you aren't sure what haircut style will work for you, try what the barber recommends. If the barber is not competent enough to pass this test, perhaps it is time for you look for another barber.

Additionally, barbers are trained to comb through the hair prior to starting any service. This allows them to look for anything that will preclude providing the sought-after style or service.

It is important that clients communicate with their barber about what they do and don't like about their hair or style. But they must be realistic. Most barbers I have spoken with say men with receding hairlines are the most difficult to service, because, for some illogical reason, they believe the hair is going to grow back.

Once you have a "meeting of the minds" with your barber and decide on the cut you desire and the barber has started on your service, avoiding changing your mind. When that occurs, most barbers will charge you for two services. That's because changing the length of a cut will necessitate cutting around the entire head all over again. A barber can become angry when a service has been accomplished according to instruction, but the client wants something else done. Also refrain from using the word *short* when describing the haircut you desire. A barber's interpretation of a short haircut is different from that of someone not in the industry.

Most barbers use professional hair-care products in a client's hair. Unless you inquire, you will never know what they are. Therefore, be very observant and ask what the product is, how much of it is being used, and its effect. Once you have asked, most barbers will show you the container, provide usage instructions, and let you know where you can purchase some.

Clients should not settle for anything less than competence, consistency, and professionalism from their barber. Sloppiness, inconsistency, gossiping, bad service, and unprofessional "haircutters" do exist. Paying customers are encouraged to help weed them out of the industry by not using their services and telling others not to either.

Leland (2009) says that many men today are missing out on the benefits of having a regular barber. As the barbershop tradition fades, men end up going to the closest unisex salon to get their haircut. Each time they go, they end up with a different stylist and are forced to explain over and over how they'd like it done. However, Leland's contentions are based on geographical, age, and ethnic assumptions. Barbers do not like chair jumpers, because every barber has a unique way of getting the same results. Using the same barber for every cut minimizes the chance of a bad haircut and maximizes the opportunity for a perfect haircut with every visit.

Good barbers have a superb memory. Once you visit a first-rate barber regularly, her or she will become familiar with the many curves of your head and your hair's texture complexities. The barber will then know how to cut and style your hair any way you desire. You will also be able to request the usual style without having to give an elaborate explanation. Most barbers are also their clients' friends; the barber becomes someone clients look forward to seeing and talking with about what has been happening since their last meeting.

But how does a man go about forging this important relationship and finding a good barber? How do you know when a barber is a keeper? Prior to entering a new shop, do the following:

- Ask around. If you're new in town or aren't happy with your current barber situation, the first thing you should do is check out the haircuts you see others wearing or ask people you know for a recommendation. Especially seek out recommendations from men who always seem to have awesome haircuts. More than likely, they have a great barber that they'd be more than happy to recommend to you.
- Search online. Check out Instagram, Facebook, and Twitter, and ask people you know for barber recommendations. Also check out what the web has to say. A recently established web based radio station, www.cutzradio.com commenced on-air operations during March 2015 and its target audience is those in the hair care industry and their clients. E-mail the station while they are on the air and the announcer will definitely give you a shout out. In order to find masculine establishments as opposed to unisex barbershops, run Google searches with keywords like *barbershop* or *(your ethnicity) barbershop*. Also, check out barbershop reviews on sites like citysearch.com and yelp.com.
- Look for confidence. When you enter a shop for the first time, look for the barber that immediately projects confidence. Look for someone who looks people in the eye when he communicates. If a barber sits on his gluteus maximums and attempts to discuss something with you, run away as fast as possible. Those barber

lacks confidence in their abilities. Perhaps they are afraid you will ask for a service can't be perform.

- Check how well groomed the barber is. Great barbers take their personal appearance seriously because they are in the business of helping men with their personal and professional image.
- Take note of the shop's cleanliness. If it looks unsanitary, look further. More than likely, if a shop is filthy, the equipment is too. Although shops are regulated for health, sanitation, and hygiene, inspectors make infrequent visits; therefore, barbers and establishment owners sometimes become very relaxed in their efforts to maintain cleanliness. Nonetheless, most seasoned barbers are independent contractors who have an eye for detail and will make sure the establishment and working areas are in good shape.
- Does the barber ask the right questions? Effective communication skills are a requirement for a master barber. A good barber should be able to ask the right questions regarding a desired service. Unskilled barbers rely on clipper guards.
- Does the barber ask for feedback during the cut? Throughout the haircutting process, a good barber communicates with clients, often by using a mirror to help the clients see the cut. This two-way communication preempts any chance for a haircut disaster. Bad or inexperienced barbers do not seek advice or feedback until they are finished and swivel the client around in the chair to look in the mirror. Often, it's much too late.
- Conduct an interview. As if hiring a new employee, conduct interviews to get a feel for whether a barber is the right person to service your hair consistently. Focus on the barber's experience and personality. To get an idea of the barber's experience, ask, "How long have you been cutting hair, and where have you barbered?" Also ask how many heads the barber cuts on the busiest day in comparison to the busiest barber in that shop. That question will shed light on the barber's competence. Barbers who are on their feet from open until close are usually excellent barbers. Finally, ask a few personality questions as well.

- Traditionally, barbers are well known for having a lot of drama in their lives. If they speak ill will of the owner or coworkers, or talk about switching shops because they're having lots of family problems, this is a warning sign that you won't be able to count on them. Barbers with lots of drama have a tendency to cancel or show up late for appointments.
- Start slowly. Of course, once you've talked to a barber, it's hard just to get up and walk out. And if you're thinking that the new barber fits the bill, you won't know for sure until he cuts your hair. The best way to figure out how skilled the barber is without risking a messed-up haircut is simply to ask that he clean up your hairline around your ear and your neck. That's hard to mess up, but if he does, it won't be noticeable.

CHAPTER EIGHT

INDUSTRY ETIQUETTE

The barbershop is a black man's country club. In past years, it was conceivable for a man to have the same barber his entire adult life. The barber is the most personal person to a man outside of his immediate family (Man Code, 2012). Your barber is not just a barber; he or she is a friend, confidante, psychologist, oracle, mind reader, or anything else you need for him or her to be that day. The barber is a creator of the look a man presents to the world. For any special event, preparation starts with a haircut. A haircut can literally change how a man feels about himself and can do wonders by boosting his confidence.

The barbershop is a microcosm of the black community. It is a place where you can be yourself and where truth is always expected. The barbershop is everything to everyone; you never know whom you are going to meet; you never know what will be discussed; and if you ever need something, someone in the barbershop is going to be able to help you or know someone that can. If you need a television, mechanic, doctor, or lawyer, or if you want to buy a house, rent a condo, get dance lessons, sell products, or buy products, you can do it all at the barbershop. The barbershop is Craigslist, eBay, USA Today, ESPN, BET, and the Yellow Pages all in one.

According to menshair.about.com n.d., the following are some simple barbershop etiquette tips that few clients are familiar with because no one has mentioned to them:

- Never question a barber about his or her sexual preference.
- Wives, girlfriends, mothers, partners, and dads, unless you are getting a haircut, please stay in the waiting area. If it's not a child's first haircut or a ritual like that, barbers don't need to have the extended family witnessing the act. Go back there only at the request of the barber. If there are hangers-on stalking the haircut, ask them to go to the waiting area so the barber doesn't have to.
- Don't coach you barber once there is a meeting of the minds.
- Unless you did not like the haircut or service, *tip your barber*. If you want to be you barber's favorite client, tip *well*.
- Don't leave a barber's tip with the receptionist.
- Don't attempt to sell you barber drugs.
- Barbers love stories, so talk all you want. Or don't talk. But whatever you do, avoid bobble heading. Your barber is on a schedule and does not have time to stop repeatedly for you to gesture. Also keep your conversation pleasant and professional.
- Don't be late for a scheduled appointment and then expect to be the next client serviced.
- Once in the chair, use your cell phone only if truly necessary.
- Don't try to become your barber's best friend. It hinders your ability to complain if you get a bad cut or poor service.
- Don't come in sweaty and stinky with product in your hair.
- Avoid wearing a hat when you plan to get a low or short cut; it makes the cut difficult to blend or taper.
- Be nice and respectful of your barber and the waiting clients.
- Don't come in boisterous and take over a conversation.

Clients should never want their barbers to consider them the customer from hell. No barber wants to deal with a customer who demeans, disrespects, or treat him or her as a subordinate. The goal for both should be a healthy relationship that lasts for years. Both can have objectives or moods that clash from time to time. Tension can develop, but the goal is to resolve it or to realize there is a mismatch and both need to go their separate ways. Often, ego gets in the way of reason, but there are barbers out there that are exceedingly talented but humble. Barbers have a difficult job. Most are on their feet all day long, while trying to make their clients look great, even if they have difficult-to-manage hair. Clients must understand that even the best barbers aren't miracle workers.

CHAPTER NINE

CAMARADERIE AND MORALE

It is important that owners or management not select individuals just because they have the required licenses. Selecting the right barber has never been more important than it is today. Matching a barber with your organizational culture is critical to creating a proper fit. Someone who is a good fit for your barbershop culture will transition easily and become a valuable asset.

A balanced barbering staff requires inclusiveness through diversity but also similar backgrounds and interests. Any misalignment of organizational culture will affect the morale and camaraderie of the staff. Keep in mind that Webster's defines *camaraderie* as mutual trust and friendship among people who spend a lot of time together. Also, establishment owners must be careful not to confuse cultural fit with discrimination.

Poor leadership in a barbershop is one of the leading killers of morale among hair-care practitioners. Barbers who have no respect for their superiors may find it difficult to take work seriously, particularly if they believe that a shop is so mismanaged that it won't be around much longer. Establishment owners who fail to clearly express expectations run the risk that their staff, which will be unsure of exactly what they should be striving for as a team, will lose morale and will stop trying altogether. Lack of personal relationships between establishment owners and barbers also can lead to a situation in which the barbers feel like numbers rather than individuals.

Setting the costs of services too low can also cause low morale. When barbers are underpaid for their craft, they feel undervalued and stressed out, and they are likely to start looking for a better position. Lack of support for continuing educational or development programs may cause recently licensed barbers to feel that they've stumbled into a dead-end job. On the other hand, barbers who feel that they are paid fairly and have access to development opportunities are more likely to feel that they are valued and part of a team.

Poor management and inadequate pay often contribute to a high turnover rate. Nothing kills camaraderie in a barbershop faster than high practitioner turnover. It's difficult to feel like part of a team and develop valuable relationships when the members of the team keep changing—especially if everyone knows it's because people are leaving in search of better work. A high rate of barber turnover encourages remaining employees to leave a shop in search of better working conditions.

Although some amount of conflict in a barbershop is unavoidable, letting conflict become the norm can kill both morale and team spirit. Avoid pitting barbers against each other; all barbers should feel that they are working together to achieve a common result. Whether you're doling out discipline or rewards, any appearance of unfairness or favoritism is the fastest way to foster resentment and drive a wedge between barbers who should be working together as a team.

Camaraderie is more than just having fun. It is also about creating a common sense of purpose and a "we're in it together" mentality. Camaraderie in a barbershop can create esprit de corps, which includes mutual respect, a common sense of identity, and admiration for hard work. Barbers also form a strong support network among each other, both personally and professionally. Establishment owners can help barbers to build rapport with one another by having breakfast meetings and discussing goals or changes in a relaxed environment.

CHAPTER TEN

MENTORSHIP

The content in this chapter was written by Wally Bock. It and Bock's other writings can viewed at http://www.agreatsupervisor.com/articles/apprenticetrade.htm#top. (Copyright 2005 by Wally Bock.)

Leadership Is an Apprentice Trade

They don't start with theory. New leaders learn leadership from more experienced leaders. That's why leadership is an apprenticeship trade. Since the Middle Ages, apprentices have learned their craft from those who have already mastered it. To get the most out of the experience, you should do a few specific things.

Role Models: Watching Others

Start by identifying excellent role models in the world around you. How do you do that? Ask. People know who the great leaders are in any organization. Once you know who they are you can use them as role models. Ask yourself, "How would Art handle this?" Think about how Grace might deal with a situation like the one you're facing. Then, adapt their behavior to fit your style and situation. Don't stop there. Maybe you haven't spotted a leader who does almost everything the way you want to. Don't let that stop you. Use one leader as a role model for one kind of behavior and another leader for a different behavior. Using role models for guidance is a start. Maybe one of your role models can become a mentor.

Mentors: Learning One-on-One

According to Greek mythology, when Odysseus left for the Trojan War, he left his son Telemachus in the care of Mentor. Mentor did an excellent job and gave his name to anyone who becomes your trusted teacher and guide.

A mentor will help you learn about leadership, taking the role that the master took in classic apprentice training systems. But a mentor will also be a guide to the larger world and often will become a good friend. Many organizations now have mentoring programs that pair up less experienced folks with people who are willing to act as mentors. Many times that doesn't work out because good mentoring relationships depend on chemistry.

Even if your organization has a mentoring program, it's probably a good idea to seek out potential mentors on your own. Here's the kind of person you should look for.

Your potential mentor should be more experienced than you in areas that matter to you. He or she should have an excellent reputation.

Your potential mentor should be a master of the organization as well as leadership. A great mentor will also become your advocate, booster and sponsor. Your potential mentor should be able to explain things well. That's important. Not everyone who can do something well can explain the details to others. You and your potential mentor should have a comfortable chemistry. There's no way to figure out in advance if this will happen, so make your approach and see how things work out.

A Framework for Learning

The best apprenticeship programs combine formal learning with learning from the masters and learning on the job. There are a number of books and training programs that will help you sort out the lessons from your learning and develop new skills in a safe environment. If you work for a large organization, take advantage of the training they have to offer. Look beyond training in "leadership" skills and try to identify any skills that will help you do your job better.

Look beyond your own organization, too. There are lots of classes in leadership and related disciplines at educational institutions. There are public seminars put on by the chamber of commerce. And trade and professional associations offer training and education of all kinds. Read a lot. Find books on leadership, management and supervision. You may find one or two that will give you the structure for your learning.

Don't just read books on the topic of leadership. Read histories and biographies that tell you about leaders of the past and present.

Trial and Feedback

Reading and courses are not enough. Leadership only happens in a group and it only happens when you do something. Learning leadership is not like learning history. It's more like learning to ride a bicycle, complete with falls and scrapes.

You'll learn your leadership trade more effectively if you critique your own leadership performance. I suggest getting a notebook and keeping a record of what you do and the results you get.

If you talk to someone who works for you about their performance, make a record of what you did and what happened. Review your notebook from time to time and use it as a guide to changed behavior, learning and development. The fact is that if you're responsible for the performance of a group, then you're a leader. You have no choice because people will treat you like a leader. The only question left is what kind of leader you'll become. To become the best leader you can, treat leadership like an apprentice trade. Learn your craft in every way you can. Find good role models and emulate their actions. Find a mentor and learn the lessons he or she has to teach. Develop a framework so you can get the most out of your learning. Finally, act and critique in an unending cycle of leadership improvement.

CHAPTER ELEVEN

SOCIAL RESPONSIBILITY

Barbershops, like all other businesses in a community, should have viable and consistent corporate social-responsibility programs. Barbershop owners should solicit participation in these programs from their booth renters. Barbers get to meet new people and become part of the community. A good place to start is in a school athletic program or domestic violence shelter. Clients are the lifeblood of any organization. Therefore, being responsible corporately is vital to sustaining the business. The following are some guidelines from Small Business (n.d.) showing a process whereby a small business could increase their business by creating social programs:

- **Set goals.** What do you want to achieve? What do you want your business to achieve? Enhance your business's image by involving the community?
- **Decide what cause you want to align yourself with.** This may be your toughest decision, considering all the option out there: children, senior citizens, homeless people, people with disabilities, military personnel—the list goes on. You might want to consider a cause that fits in with your service where you may get a return on your investments. Another way to narrow the field is by considering not only causes you feel strongly about, but also those that your customer base considers significant.

- **Where possible, choose a nonprofit or other organization to partner with.** Get to know the group, and make sure it's sound, upstanding, geographically convenient, and willing to cooperate with you in developing a partnership.
- **Design a program, and propose it to the nonprofit group.** Besides laying out what you plan to accomplish, also include indicators that will measure the program's success in tangible terms.
- **Negotiate an agreement with the organization.** Know what they want before you sit down, and try to address their concerns up front. Seek their collaboration.
- **Involve employees.** Unless you get employees involved from the beginning, they won't be able to connect fully and communicate the real caring involved in the campaign to customers.
- **Involve customers.** Don't just do something good and tell your customers about it later. Get customers involved, too? Make it easy for customer to do well; then reward them for doing it. A great way to show social responsibility is by annually holding a customer appreciation day providing free food and having events for all age categories.

According to Levin (2011), some barbershops aren't just for haircuts anymore. The old-fashioned, conventional barbershops that are still pillars in neighborhoods that house large minority populations may be the catalyst for a new role: serving as stations for health care in their sector of society.

The barbershop is not just a place to get a haircut; it has long been a place for gathering and a place for social and political interaction. In African American and Latino cultures, men congregate to sit and talk for thirty minutes. It's almost like free therapy sessions, contends Levin, and there are few other places like it. Barbershops have long been men's sanctum.

The barbershop's role as an addition to the health care system began in California with screening for hypertension and diabetes and has since expanded elsewhere in the United States.

Releford et al. (2010) says that the Black Barbershop Health Outreach Program (BBHOP) has become a rapidly growing phenomenon. Clinicians established BBHOP to enhance community-level awareness of and empowerment to combat cardiometabolic disorders such as diabetes and cardiovascular disease. This program is among several successful outreach programs sought to promote health through barbershops.

CHAPTER TWELVE

ESTABLISHMENT OWNER'S PERSPECTIVE

I had an opportunity to interview what youngsters in the hair-care industry call "old-school barbers." It's understandable why John Olivas relishes the title: he was either the younger barbers' instructor at Rooston's School of Hair Design or their instructor in the San Bernardino Adult School barber preapprenticeship course.

John entered the industry under the apprenticeship program in 1965 after being discharged from the Marine Corps (personal communication, July 7, 2014). He opened his own shop in 1999. John noted he obtained his barber instructor's license in 1973, became the primary instructor for the San Bernardino Adult School, and has been teaching there since. Additionally, John owned and operated the Rooston's School of Hair Design from 1985 to 2010, where he was the instructor for eighteen months before opening a barber supply store. As you can see, hair care is in his blood.

I asked John to elaborate on how the hair-care industry has changed since he first started barbering. He said that barbers from the sixties and seventies took barbering seriously and considered it a profession. He contended that many of those entering the industry today—both men and women—look at it as only a job. "There was pride in work and generous corporate social responsibility within the community," he said. "Today's barbers do not feel they have any attachment to the community other than barbering." John added that that there were two separate boards to regulate the industry, but the state government decided to merge them. Within a few years after the merger, the image of the industry began to change. Barbers began to lose pride in their workmanship.

John said camaraderie within the industry has taken a big hit; it is nonexistent. He contended that barbers used to socialize, communicating with their competitors to keep the prices and quality of service up. He said that no longer happens because it is all about the money; that is why you see price wars just to get business. He felt that the way some barbers dress is disgraceful (such as sagging), and he said it's no wonder they consistently have to cut walk-ins. The industry as a whole has become too casual, John contended.

The interview shifted to contrasting and comparing the training received now and attending a regular barber school or an apprenticeship program. John said that an apprenticeship program is better because the apprentice gets to earn money while he or she learns the craft. Apprentices are in a regular shop, so they learn what the customers' needs are and what type of equipment and products are required to fill those needs. In addition, an apprentice gets to cut more heads on a day-to-day basis than a regular student, who is limited mainly because of management's failure to market.

Another of John's concerns was that many cosmetologists are crossing over to barbering, which can hurt the industry as well. Those who have been working in the cosmetology field for a while seem reluctant to learn all the characteristics of operation and barbering in a full-scale salon. John said that all they want to do is learn how to cut hair. However, many cosmetologists with less experience are hungry and enthusiastic about learning the finer aspects of men's grooming.

John and I discussed racial and gender diversity relative to the hiring of a barber as well as servicing clients of different ethnicities. He said that since barbershops have abandoned the residential neighborhood, an establishment owner has no choice but to embrace diversity. Men are no longer the only family income earners. Many women are entering the industry, and some work harder and therefore become better practitioners than their male counterparts. "Some barbers lack the skills of cutting the various types of hair and doing what is necessary to become proficient with the straight razor," John said. Versatility breeds more income. "The clientele in my shop is diverse, and I would embrace the hiring of any barber that is a reflection of the clientele base," he added.

Just as the barbershop abandoned the residential neighborhood, many of the longtime neighbors relocated as well. Neighborhood barbershops used to be built to accommodate two or three stations. Now, for a barbershop to sustain itself, its must be able to accommodate seven or more workstations. John is of the opinion that there should be some seasoned barbers to teach the younger barbers, adding diversity to a shop. In doing so, the staff is capable of performing any service a client desires.

CHAPTER THIRTEEN

PRACTITIONER'S PERSPECTIVE

Reggie Ferguson, a former establishment owner and now a barber at the Rico's in Murrieta, California, got into the hair-care industry in 1992 at the age of twenty-one while residing in Norfolk, Virginia (personal interview, July 9, 2014). He said that smoking was allowed in barbershops, and the booth rent was much cheaper than today. Reggie said that cutting hair has always been his passion. He cut hair throughout high school, and it upset him that no one from the industry came to the school to talk to the kids about it becoming their profession. Furthermore, he said that barbering has been good to him. In 1998, at the age of twenty-six, Reggie relocated to San Diego from North Carolina and opened a barbershop. He said that time brought on many changes for the betterment of the industry. For example, social media has enhanced barbers' ability to market their skills. Additionally, for years cosmetologists had the hair market cornered. Now barbers throughout the country attend hair shows specifically for barbers. Reggie said he would be a shop owner again, now that he has found the blueprint for success. He highly recommended entering the industry at a young age because it allows you to learn from those with more experience, and you will be able to grow in the business. "As a barber, you are your own boss, and you have the flexibility to work your desired schedule. However, if you don't work, you don't earn any money." Reggie said that barbers are a different class of people. You find some that are lazy when it comes to replacing their merchandise and equipment. Many barbers just borrow from others rather than buy their own. “I believe that is a reflection of one’s upbringing,” he said.

When Reggie was residing on the East Coast, he saw one female barber. He said that, after moving to San Diego, “I didn’t see any female barbers. It was not until I relocated to Murrieta that I started seeing more female barbers. Those that work with me can definitely hold their own and then some.” He believes that establishment owners in each region should meet to establish prices for various services and designate days when all shops will be closed. Doing so would eliminate the chop shops that frequently undercut other establishments. Meeting would be a win-win for all concerned because barber unions are a thing of the past. (For a sample of Reggie’s haircutting ability, see figure 13.1 below.)

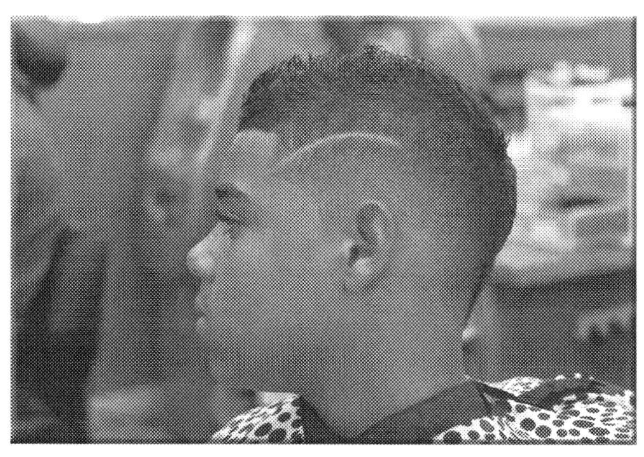

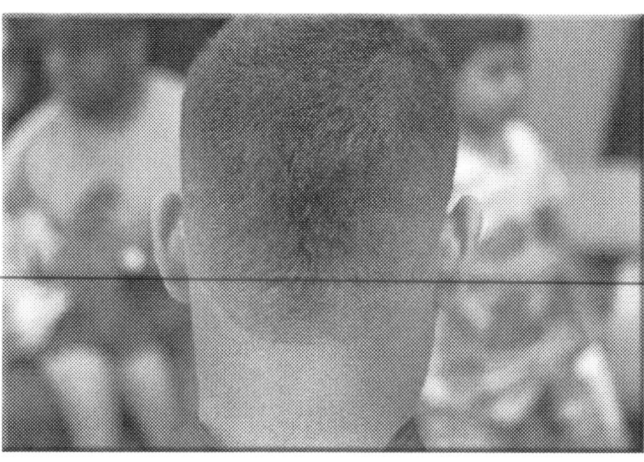

One of Rico's barber apprentices, Jason Williams, described how well he was able to assimilate with Team Rico after receiving his apprenticeship license (personal conversation, July 5, 2014). He said it was not a difficult process; his focus was mainly on learning and adjusting to the personalities of each barber as well as watching their haircutting techniques.

> I find that each barber has certain little things that they do different from others. I try to engage myself with some of the things they do in order to master my own individual style. Team Rico accepted me into the fold unconditionally, based on my persistence to get it right and being an attentive listener when being provided guidance. Learning the shop's etiquette was not a problem, because I was provided a lengthy shop policy letter upon entering the apprenticeship program. However, I find the industry etiquette varies from shop to shop.

Jason added that he continuously works on the art of communicating with clients while learning both good and bad habits of a barber. (See a sample of Jason's artistically ability in figure 13.2 below.)

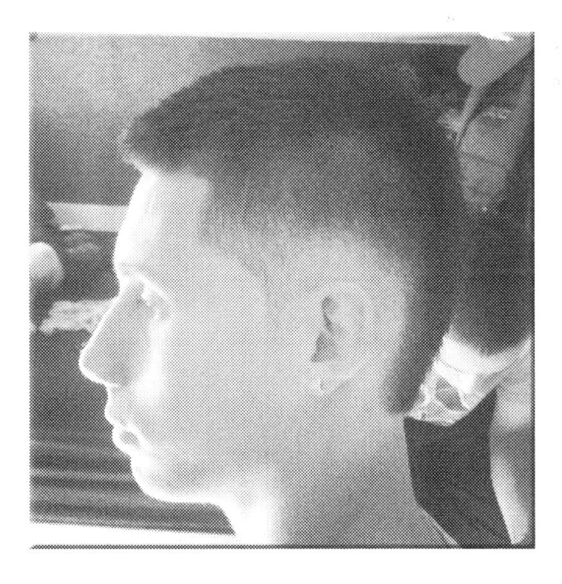

Liz Ouintero, one of the female barbers I interviewed, said she really enjoys working at Rico's, mainly because of the environment; she considers all her coworkers to be an extended family (personal interview, July 2, 2014). She also said that any woman working in a predominately male-oriented environment is going to be hit on and approached in various manners by clients, adding that she has no problems with her male coworkers. I asked how she dealt with it. "I tell them straight that I am married with two daughters and I am 100 percent devoted and dedicated to my husband," she replied. She further iterated that always communicating with a smile prevents alienating the client, while at the same time she tells him she enjoys having him as a client and servicing his hair but their relationship must remain professional. She added, "Otherwise they can choose one of the other eleven barbers."

Liz said that working in the industry allows her more control over her time, especially when it comes to her family. "It's important when you have young school-age kids that you don't expect the teacher to raise your child. The flexibility allows me to be home and provide my girls help with schoolwork. On nonpeak business days, I can take off to spend time with family. My clients usually call me in advance for an appointment to minimize their wait time." Appointments in barbershops are a new concept. However, some clients refuse to get on board with it, and that is fine.

Liz concluded by saying,

> I have truly learned a lot working in a barbershop, mostly good but some bad. However, I choose to focus on the good because it allows me to evaluate things from a man's perspective, especially when dealing with my husband … I never realized that a good barber is also a psychologist, because one must be a good and attentive listener … Most clients, as soon as they sit, have something to share that's going on in their life, and they are seeking their barber's opinion.

(See Liz's artistic styling in figures 13.3 and 13.4 below.)

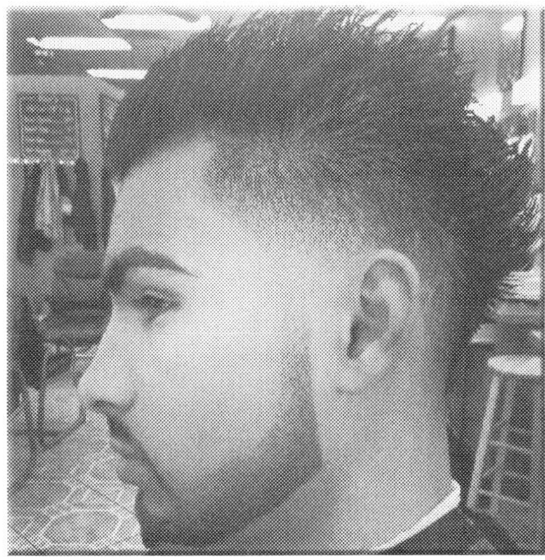

One of the original Rico's barbers, Laron Harvey, who has been in the industry for more than ten years. He said in a personal interview (July 22, 2014) that his first opportunity to enter the industry was back home in Indiana. After he relocated to Southern California, the diversity within the industry enhanced his obsession for the craft. While working as a haircutter, Laron was introduced to me, and I encouraged him to do it the right way and get licensed. He entered the apprenticeship program and was licensed as a master barber within two years.

Laron reluctantly noted that his passion for the field forced him to be a "haircutter" prior to being sanctioned legally with a state license. He was inspired to become a barber because, as a child, he fell in love with what he perceived as the lifestyle of a barber. After being pressed to be more specific, he asserted that a barber is "a strong and important person within the community who displays passion for the craft."

Laron said that the hair-care industry will continue to grow and progress over the next twenty years. He expected it to get back to where it once was when men really cared about how their hair looked. He also said his contribution to the industry will be in the form of giving back and sharing the knowledge and technical expertise that was given to him.

A typical workday for Laron is good and easy; he relaxes and keeps an open mind to further enhance his talent in the art of hairstyles and designs. He said that he grooms himself well in preparation for grooming others. "In doing so, it puts me in a positive mind frame to take care of my clients and make them look as good as I possibly can."

Laron said that a typical workweek for him can be physically draining because of the length of time he has to stand; some days he goes without taking a lunch break. Sometimes it can be an aching back while other times his feet hurt. That's why it is important to be very selective of the shoes you choose to wear. However, from a financial point of view, at the end of the week, the profession is very promising and rewarding.

Laron contended that the most challenging part of his job is dealing with clients who have bad attitudes or come in with a chip on their shoulder, looking for a confrontation. Over time, he has learned how to deal with them without being disrespectful. Energy and mood is a key dynamic when dealing with rude clients. "I take it as a challenge," he said. "I try my best to give them the best haircut they ever had. In this business, the client's experience is the most important feature towards being satisfied."

He added, "The most enjoyable component of my job is watching a client smile with gratitude after getting a great cut—and my ability to help someone have a better day." He also said that the camaraderie among his peers is immeasurable. "We are family, and it starts with management."

Laron said that the overall culture has become more diverse and hip-hop. This change can be attributed to social media and the Gen X and Y individuals entering the field, which is wide open for anyone with good hand-eye coordination; the opportunities are boundless as demand continues to increase. On the other hand, Laron said, many are leaving the field through attrition due to retirement; physical ailments; not making enough money; the emotional ups and downs life presents; an unwillingness to hone the craft; or lack of clientele.

If he was forced to change anything about his career pattern, Laron said it would be to change how he handles his finance. His current working condition is far better than at any of the other places he worked, mostly because of the environment, management, location, energy, setup, and interior decoration. "I learned within two months that barbers must determine for themselves if they are a fit for an establishment."

Laron said the most challenging part of his job is the long days and not being able to rest. The most rewarding part of his job is watching his younger clients grow into adolescence, seeing smiles after haircuts, and growing as a barber himself. He concluded, "I get two weeks off a year, and often I don't use it. My future plan is to start taking more time off to enjoy the fruits of my labor." (See one of Laron's cuts in figure 13.5 below.)

Another Rico's team member is Akeele Pearson, who has been in the industry professionally and legally a little over three years (personal interview, July 26, 2014). As with many of the licensed practitioners, he was a haircutter long before entering barbering industry. Akeele said the passion for cutting hair and seeing the final results motivated him toward becoming a licensed barber. It thrilled him to see the joy conveyed by clients after they received a nice, fresh haircut. He noted his gratitude to me for giving him his first opportunity to work in a licensed establishment.

Akeele said the industry has been strengthening, and he foresees it continuing in that path over the next several years. This trend can be attributed to the advent and improvement of the Internet along with social media. In addition, many in the industry initially thought of barbering as a job, but it soon became their passion; money became secondary. Akeele said that his contribution to the improvement and success of the industry will be that of providing technical advice and assistance to licensed practitioner.

"A typical work day for me is busy," Akeele said. "Though at the end of the week I am physically drained and exhausted, financially it is rewarding and joyful. In this industry you are constantly standing and grinding." He finds the different textures of hair to be the most difficult part of his job. "I attribute this difficulty to my limited time in the industry and lack of exposure," he said. Notwithstanding the fact that as a new barber you are hesitant to try cutting textures of hair you are not familiar with. The hesitation relates to lack of confidence in your ability or afraid that if you do not attain the desired results your peers will criticize you.

"The most enjoyable part of my job is customer service, knowing and meeting the satisfaction of myself, client and peers. There are no limitations when it comes to customer service. The customer is always and in all ways right."

Akeele said the barbering culture in general has become toxic for several reasons:

- Establishment owners allow unlicensed individuals to portray themselves as licensed practitioners. (It's the invasion of the haircutters!)
- Licensed barbers agree to work in establishments with unlicensed individuals.
- Cosmetologist cross over to the field for the sake of making a quick dollar.
- Licensed barbers lack passion for the industry.
- Licensed barbers with less skill lower their prices to undercut their coworkers for the sake of getting a client to sit in their chair.
- Licensed barbers are not interested in continuing education as long as they can pay their rent.
- Licensed barbers have no patience with struggling barbers and lack a desire to help them with the finer aspects of the craft.

Akeele said that one of the reasons people leave the industry is because of the challenge of dealing with different people. Some also lack patience to build a reputable clientele base. He further asserted that Rico's is a multicultural and diverse shop and is one of the best spots to be in to learn all aspects of a barbering operation because management does not withhold information about the business side.

Akeele said, "Since being on Team Rico's, I've learned the turn-on and turn-off mode of shop operation. Conversations in barbershops can sometimes become not too pleasing to the ears of some clients; therefore, knowing those modes is important. Barbers on Team Rico don't just cut hair, they also get an education on both business and life skills." He added, "The most challenging aspect of my job is making people happy. Sometimes that can be a tough sell."

The advice Akeele would give to anyone considering in becoming a barber is to be patient, know what you want to do in your lifetime, and make sure you're happy and eager to come to work every day. "You have to want to be at the shop; don't bring your problems to work, because many of your clients are waiting to discuss their problems with you." Akeele concluded by saying every barber should have the goal of operating his or her own shop someday. (See his work in figure 13.6 below.)

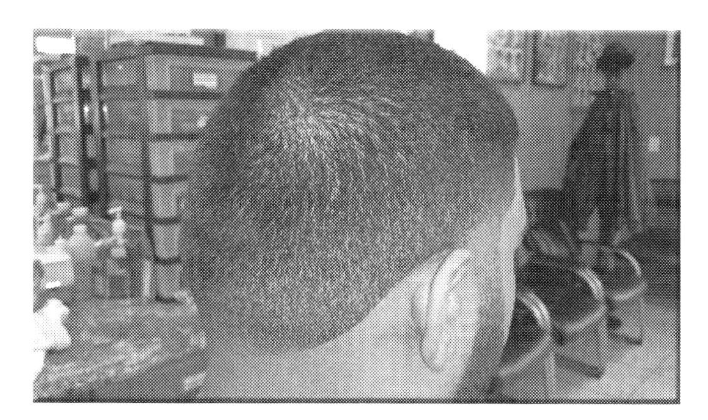

Derek Sanders has been in the hair-care industry professionally for approximately nine years (personal interview, July 28, 2014). He said his inspiration for becoming a barber was that it required attention to detail toward transforming the looks of a client. "Prior to entering the field, I felt it would be a vocation that I could become passionate with,"

he said. "I just enjoyed the atmosphere and friendship of warmth where I used to go get my haircut."

Derek is of the opinion that the industry will expand tremendously in the area of marketing. In recent years, the Internet has already become a valuable tool, allowing barbers to display their talent globally. "I foresee the industry having awards shows on the scale of the GRAMMYs," he said. "My contribution to the industry is to continue marketing myself by using social media and helping less-experience barbers understand that barbering is not a job, it is a customer-based profession or business."

Derek said his typical workday consists of going to the gym for a workout. "The daily exercise routine helps to clear my mind and provides the extra pep required to get me through a day of standing. Afterward, I have breakfast then groom myself in preparation to service my clients. How can someone expect a client to seek the service if the barber is not groomed or properly attired?"

Derek continued, "At some point, well before I get to the shop, I check my telephone for appointments or scheduling changes for the day. Make every effort is made to arrive at the shop thirty minutes prior to operational hours or my first appointment, whichever comes first. This allows me to make sure I have all the products I need to service my clients and to make sure all my tools are working properly."

He added, "At the end of the week, I must say that I am physically exhausted, but pretty pleased with the monetary outcome. The most challenging aspect of my job is dealing with a disgruntled client; I must be creative in how I defuse the situation without alienating the client. On the other end of the spectrum, the most enjoyable thing about my job is the flexibility in making my schedule and deciding when to take a vacation."

Derek sees the culture of the local barbering community as complacent, though it is evolving through trend setting. "The only negative aspect of barbering is when one allows his outside personal life to interfere. For example, you are out on the town socializing, and you are an innocent bystander to a confrontation—and a shop client mistakes you for being involved. The rumor of your involvement somehow gets back to the shop, which could create a financial setback." (See samples of Derek's professional competence in figure 13.7 below.)

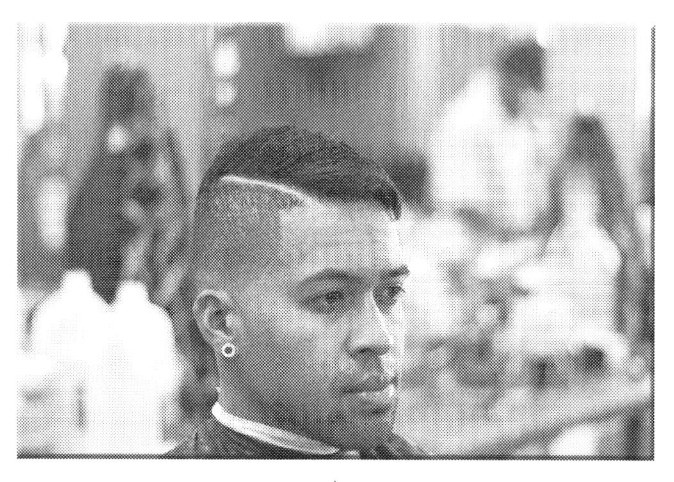

According to Derek, there are too many entering the barbering profession coupled with cosmetologists' crossing over within the industry. Many entering the profession are doing so for the wrong reason; most look at it as quick money, not realizing all that is required to maintain their tools.

In some areas of the county, you find multiple shops within a block, most competing for a target audience instead of seeking to diversify their staff and clientele base. Derek said, "Some people leave the industry because they are burned out or for medical reasons, or because they no longer desire to put the time and investment into the field. If the opportunity had presented itself, I would have entered the hair-care industry much earlier."

Derek said, "Rico's team has a specific type of bond … You can keep it real and not be offended. The team looks to grow while becoming financial solvent, taking pride in our work, and keeping the community happy with how we perform our services."

A new barber entering a multi-chair shop, regardless of experience, should not expect to be immediately accepted or welcomed by everyone. He or she must be patient and work at becoming a fit with the other barbers. Acceptance by management doesn't mean being automatically received by the mass. To gain acceptance, a new barber must be open-minded and kindhearted, listen attentively to what is being said (not how it is said), and welcome constructive criticism.

Derek said, "The most rewarding thing about my job is the satisfaction that a client would trust your judgment enough to sit in your chair and allow you to style their his the way you want without any instruction. At this stage of my life, I take off two days a week, and that is sufficient for me now. However, as I get older, I may need more time. Only time will tell." Derek's short-term goals are to increase his value and worth as a barber, increase his clientele, and stay current on trends and styles. His long-term goal is to operate his own barber establishment. (See samples of Derek's professional competence in figure 13.8.)

Jenny Oseguera has been in the barbering field for five years (personal conversation, July 24, 2014). Although she's the mother of two boys, she said she was never inspired to cut their hair until she decided to cut hair professionally. "I was inspired to become a barber mainly as a means to support my kids," she said. She was in the police academy and was injured. While recovering, her boys convinced her not to return to the police academy, and they introduced her to the barbershop owner. The rest is history!

Jenny said that since she has been in the industry, she has seen it progress, and she foresees it growing further during the next few years. As the industry grows, she would like her contribution to be becoming an establishment owner so she can provide opportunities like those given for her.

A typical workday for Jenny is one that is simply busy. She gets to meet people and "chop it up." However, at the end of the week, she feels drained and lacks energy. On the other hand, she feels financially blessed and able to purchase things for her kids, which she was not able to do before. "The most challenging part of the job is listening to the sad stories," Jenny said. "At times I find myself more of a psychologist or therapist than a barber. I have to find that balance between listening and offering a recommendation to resolve the dilemma. The most enjoyable part of my job is when I am cutting a kid's hair. I get zoned out in my own world and get to meditate about my life situations." She added,

> There is always room for more good barbers. There is enough business for everybody. An individual's personality will attract certain people. The ones that don't sit in your chair, you don't want them as a client anyway. On the other hand, some barbers leave the field because of burnout or lack of passion. My passion was to become a homicide detective; however, I will not change the path God has placed before me. It has allowed me to become passionate about cutting and styling hair.
>
> It is a blessing I was able to start my barbering career in a shop where both management and my team members treat each other with respect in a family atmosphere. It was about a month before I realized I was an acceptable fit for the team. Each barber has his or her own way of sizing a new member up. The most rewarding thing about my job is the flexibility; it affords me to be able to be there for my kids during special events, to take off for an hour to prepare my kids' evening meal then be home by seven.

(See samples of Jenny's haircuts in figure 13.8 below.)

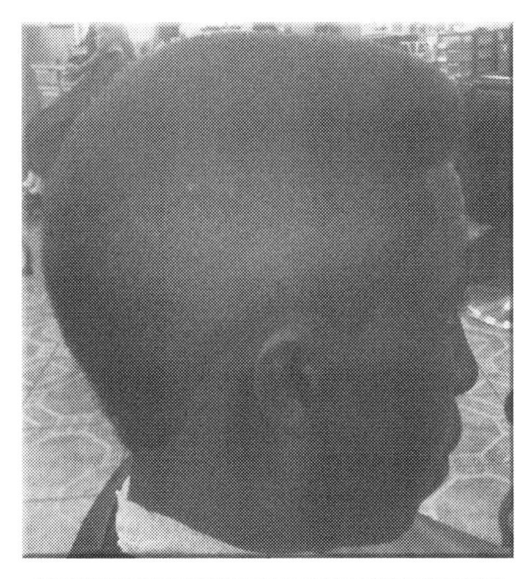

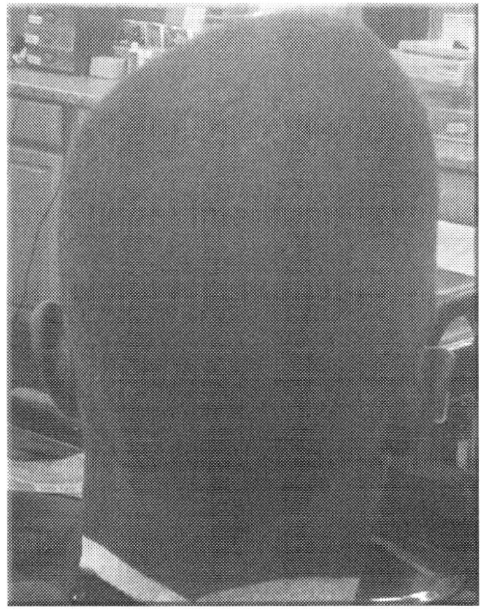

I also interviewed Cleveland Burnley, who grew up and within the hair-care industry. His mother is a cosmetologist and one of my former employees. Cleve worked as a sweeper and bar helper where his mother worked. Upon graduating from high school, he entered the barber apprenticeship program and has since become a mainstay in Team Rico. He has been licensed as a master barber for more than three years. For him, making people look good is gratifying, as he continually seeks to grow artistically.

Cleve said that barbering has always been the profession he wanted to pursue, even though his mother had other aspirations for him. According to him, his mother felt that those in the hair-care industry had to hustle to make a decent living. She preferred that he entered a profession where he would have a paycheck.

Cleve said that he has never worked in any other shop, so he would not be able to make a comparison from an employee point of view. However, he is of the opinion that there is no competition between the barbers. Everyone is on the same page, making an effort to build the shop's reputation and bring more clients into the shop.

Cleve said the most difficult part of his job is dealing with unruly kids or kids that won't be still. "For the amount we charge, parents expect their children's hair to be perfect, and it takes twice as long to service a child as an adult." He added that at the end of the workweek he is exhausted, but the money he earns makes it all worth it. He said he would love to attend hair shows, but his part-time job precludes him from doing so.

Cleve said, "The most enjoyable thing about my job is the ability to listen to music all day, to make people look good, and to joke around with the other barbers." According to him, people are leaving the barbering field because they are tired of having to hustle. The field is still basically male oriented; however, women are rapidly closing the gap. Cleve said he has no problem working with women. "Initially, I thought it was going to be stressful with drama or, more importantly, distracting if they look good." He added,

> I have adjusted to Rico's adult culture just by observing others and expressing my views, even if they are

unpopular. I believe I gained 100 percent acceptance after a year, when I cut my first clean skin fade. I would like to see the shop explode with all the social media and become known not just in this area but coast-to-coast. I have been marketing myself via social media, and it has paid off but not as much as I would like for it to.

If an unruly client disrespected the establishment or me, I would not hesitate to ask them to leave the premises. Recently, I had to remove an intoxicated client in the middle of his haircut for unruly behavior.

(See a sample of his work in figure 13.9 below.)

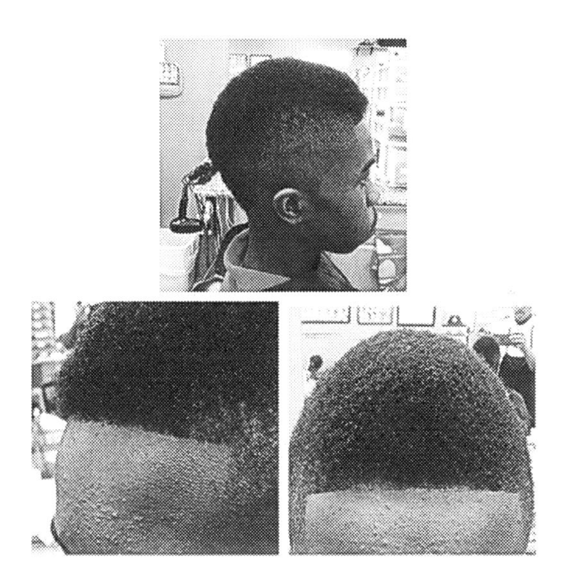

Melvin Roundtree Jr. is a barber apprentice (personal interview, September 4, 2014). He said he was cutting at an early age and became passionate about it, so he decided to make it a career. When I interviewed him, he said acted as a haircutter out of his parents' garage until he was accepted into the program. He had always had a passion for the hair-care industry but was never in a good position to pursue it until his parents communicated to me their desire to get him out of their garage and into a legitimate barbershop.

According to Melvin, the most challenging part of his job as a barber is making a concerted effort to please each and every client that sits in his chair. "It is extremely important that you give each client exactly what he or she asks for. The most rewarding part of my job is seeing the expression on clients' faces after I have worked hard to make sure they are pleased. A great haircut brings a smile on a man's face and makes him feel a little bit better about himself."

He continued,

> Because I am an apprentice in my shop, the entire master barbering staff provides me little pointers in an effort to help me get to the next level. If I need assistance or have a specific question about how to do something or work with a new technique, I ask. My trainer and I communicate on a frequent basis. Some things have been eluding me, and I am slowly getting a grasp on them. I don't worry too much about the barbering aspect; I want to learn the operational business side of things, so that one day I will be able to operate an establishment.

According to Melvin, one must be cautious when entering a new establishment as the new kid on the block. "You must feel out your coworkers and listen more than you talk, and you will be accepted as a fit sooner than you think. Prior to being licensed, I would come by and visit the shop to build camaraderie with the fellows so when I did get the license, it made my transition much easier. I was informed as to what to expect and what not to expect. I felt accepted after a week in the shop."

Melvin said it took him almost four months to get comfortable with cutting straight hair. He believes straight hair is much more forgiving than curly or nappy hair. When he first got his license, he shied away from straight-haired clients, and now his confidence has been lifted to a point that he feels capable of cutting any type of hair. Melvin is of the opinion that as he remains in the hair-care profession, being exposed and permitted to cut all textures of hair various exposure will enhance his professional capabilities.

A typical workday for Melvin is getting to work early and marketing by passing out a few business cards at surrounding business. Then he makes sure he has all the items needed for the workday and confirms his appointments for the day. Melvin does not consider cutting hair work. "Sitting between appointments or waiting for a client is more of a working situation than cutting hair," he said. "I am exhausted at the end of the week, but the financial reward makes it all worthwhile." Although "Mel Man," as he prefers to be call, is an apprentice, you can see his excellent work in figure 13.10 below.

Jim Beavan Jr., a licensed cosmetologist, transitioning to the barber side of hair care and has been licensed for three years (personal interview, September 11, 2014). He joined Team Rico about two weeks ago. His prior experience was at one of the national chain salons, which required all haircuts to be performed systematically and within a structured time frame. Jim said he's aspiring to become a barber because he excels more when cutting men's hair. He also felt that by joining an established team, he has an opportunity to take his techniques and abilities to the next level.

Jim said there was no competition among his former coworkers. However, he felt he was competing against himself as he viewed others' work and strived to do better by meeting or exceeding any and all expectations. He has never attended a hair show or barber competition.

Jim also believes work within the hair-care industry behind the chair is hard. At the end of the week, he has backaches, his feet hurt, and he sometimes has pain in his wrist. "But the work is nothing compared to construction or other strenuous occupations," he said him. "At the end of the day, it all balances out from a monetary point of view."

Jim said,

> The most enjoyable thing about my job is striving to get ahead of the learning curve. Barbering has become so artistic, and it keeps your mind moving to stay abreast of the new and various styles and techniques. The most challenging part of my job is being able to communicate often and effectively with my client while at the same time concentrate on the job at hand. Remember, I am crossing over from a cosmetologist to a barber, where the techniques are totally different and not interchangeably. Getting more comfortable with what I'm doing and more time will fix that problem.

Jim added that Rico's culture is very relaxed but remains professional. He felt that he had adjusted well and felt very comfortable with the team. The culture is stress-free, not like working for a national chain salon, where everything was structured. Jim said that if the opportunity presented itself, he would not change his career path. His past job treated both workers and clients as if they were numbers; it was f a corporate culture, creating stress for the workforce. He said, "Joining Team Rico's is a breath of fresh air. Management allows you to be yourself as long as it is within the established guidelines."

Jim utilizes social media to his advantage by sending out blasts to his local followers about his availability for cutting hair on particular days. He also gives deals as an incentive to come in for a service. He said he would not service a client that does not respect him or the shop. He also stated that he would not work in a shop with an unlicensed person. (See Jim's work in figure 13.11 below.)

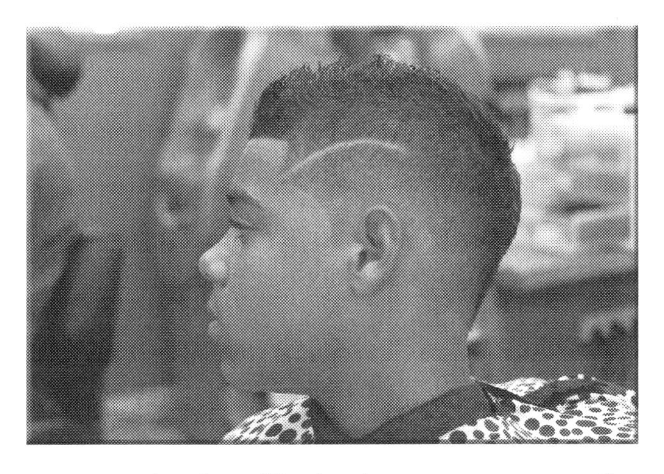

Ashley Sarian considers herself to be the consummate professional; she has been cutting hair since age fourteen (personal interview, September 11, 2014). Ashley said she was destined to be in the hair-care industry; her grandfather was a barber and operated his shop in Fallbrook, California. During visits as a child, "I would sit and watch my grandpa cut hair all day," she said. "When I was about the age of fourteen, he would allow me to try my hand at the craft, contingent upon approval of the clients. After a couple of summers passed, I fell in love with the art of making people look good. At that point and time in my life, I knew what my career path would entail."

Ashley is the latest addition to Team Rico. She has been a licensed hair care practitioner since 2006 and has a license to practice barbering in California and as a cosmetologist in Arizona. In addition to her hair-care credentials, she is also licensed as a makeup and design artist.

According to Ashley, one must have a passion to be a barber; she feels that being among barbers is like being with family. "When I'm in the shop, it's like home to me."

But her experience has not always been that good.

> I have worked in various shops, and in some barbershops, everyone is out for themselves, and no camaraderie or competition can be found. I have been in situations where I became a target purely based on my gender. However, Team Rico barbers work as a unit with one common goal, and that is to help bring out the best one has to offer. Upon joining Team Rico's, I immediately felt welcome, not because of my gender, but because of what I bring to the table in the areas of competence and professionalism.
>
> I find the culture of Rico's is different than any place I've ever worked. The organization is operated professionally. Everyone respects each other and never attempts to cheat on walk-ins. You come to work, do your job, and go home drama-free.
>
> As a female in this male-dominated profession, you can't depend on your looks or personality; as a barber, you must bring some substance. Often men would prefer women to cut their hair for the sake of being touched by the opposite gender. However, if you show competence in your work, you will have no problem building a clientele.

Ashley has been invited to cut hair for artists at the BET Awards, MTV Awards, ESPY Awards, and Hip Hop Awards.

She said she constantly attends hair shows so that she can stay abreast of the changes and styles that pops up from coast to coast.

> As a barber, you can never stop learning; when you do, your career in the hair industry has ended. A typical workweek can be different; there are various variables, such as weather, time of the month, summer months, etc. There are times when one may sit and wait, and other times when you can't take a break. In this business, you have to make the money while the iron is hot.
>
> The most challenging part of my job is that midday period when you have to wait for school to let out or for clients to get off from work. It's difficult to remain positive during that period. I challenge myself to seek ways to be creative with marketing my skills. You have to do it! It's all about you.
>
> The most enjoyable part of my job is the clients I get to meet and seeing the smile I bring to their face when I finish servicing their hair. You don't just cut their hair; you get to know them and their families through conversation. You build relationships, and that is more important than a good haircut. Some barbers leave the field because it requires patience, persistence, and professionalism. If you can't deliver on the three Ps, you are doomed from the onset.

Ashley said that barbering is a male-dominated occupation and always will be. "The barbershop is their sanctum sanatorium, and no matter how many female barbers enter the field, the percentages will never surpass that of males. As a women, you can't be thin-skinned or have rabbit ears. You must adapt, and the male barbers will protect and respect you as one of their own."

Ashley added that when men started to become cosmetologists and makeup artists, women fell in love with having a man do their hair and makeup. Flip the situation and you find that older men enjoy getting their hair-care needs met by a woman. According to her, shopping centers need to be promoted more, which is incumbent on each individual barber.

"If I was afforded an opportunity to change my career path, I would not even consider it," Ashley said. "Barbering is in my blood. I realized it was a fit and was accepted by my coworkers after my first haircut. The owner gave me one of his clients, and everyone else sat around and watched me. Once they saw the final results, they realized I could hold my own. I felt accepted. In addition, I got invited to their parties; I feel if they wanted to hang out with me after work, that means they might like me just a little bit."

Ashley said she would never work in a barbershop with someone who is unlicensed. She also said she gets hit on a lot by clients.

> I have a natural reaction that deters those types of discussion. Often a client will make a subtle comment and see how far he can go. I just shut him down right away before it gets too far. Give them a good haircut, and they will come back. You have to master how to let them down easy without [making them feel] embarrassed or rejected. I treat unruly or filthy-mouthed clients similarly. If I can't handle it, either management or one of my fellow barbers will have to deal with it. If there are other women considering the barbering profession, I want to let you know it's hard, but don't give up. Stick with it and reap the monetary rewards.

(See a sample of Ashley's haircutting skills in figure 13.12 below.)

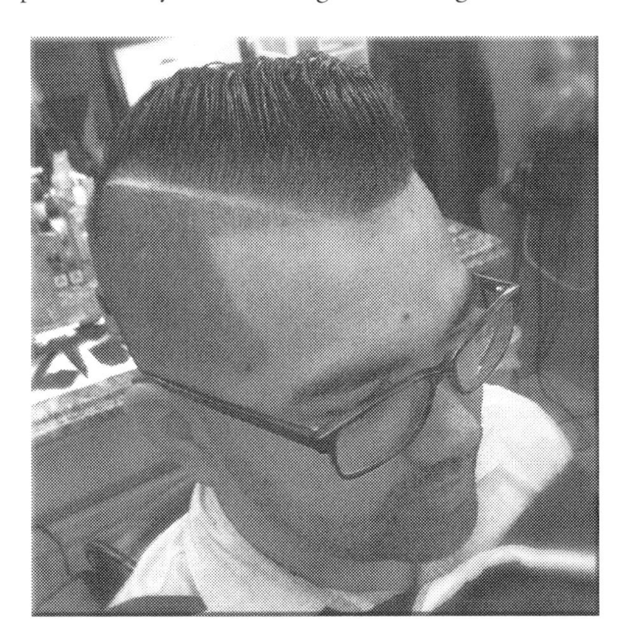

Ian Fleming has been barbering for almost eight years (personal interview, December 30, 2014). He was a barber apprentice at the original Rico's and considers himself one of the original Team Rico members. He said he got into barbering because of the fast money. "You are your own boss and, more importantly, the independent aspect of it. There has always been competition among the barbers at Rico's as it relates to who has the most clients or cuts the best or quickest. That is one of the hallmarks for keeping your job. If you do not perform up to par, you will lose your clients faster than you got them."

Ian said he attends hair shows to stay abreast of the many changes in haircuts, styles, and designs. "For a log period of time, I was the only one in my shop doing designs, and now … almost everyone is doing them. When attending a hair show, you also learn other techniques and the different tools being used to obtain the ultimate results that you seek in your designs.

Ian said that there is a lot of brotherhood and camaraderie among barbers. He gets to meet people from all walks of life, nationalities, and ethnicities that he would never have been associated with in a traditional environment. A typical workday for him is ten to twelve hours because of his personal telephone application; his clients can schedule their own appointments without communicating personally with him. "From a financial point of view, it couldn't be better, because I get money every day," he said. He added,

> The most challenging part of the job is dealing with the clients' attitudes and personalities. However, on the flipside of that, the most enjoyable part of the job is that you are your own boss, and the only person you have to satisfy is your client, because that is who pays you. Some people can't make it in this field because of the intimidation factor from both clients and coworkers, the frustration of not being able to cut as well as the other barbers, or the inability to maintain a clientele base to support yourself.

Ian said that barbers that move around from shop to shop find themselves on the outside looking in because "clients will not follow you even if it is across the street." According to Ian, barbering is still a male-dominated field. However, the few women he has worked with "can carry their weight." There are many who prefer to have women cut their hair.

Ian said that he didn't adjust to the Rico's culture; since he was with the original crew, he helped to create that culture. Management created a structure to go by, and he hasn't wavered a bit from that—and it is working. Meaning no drugs, fighting, smoking, or loitering! Ian said, "I am so pleased with the people I work with and how the establishment is operated. If I were afforded an opportunity to choose a different career path, I would decline in a heartbeat. I realized I was a fit for the rest of the crew after I was on the apprenticeship program about three months. I enjoy making people look good after a fresh cut, which is the most enjoyable part of barbering."

Ian said he uses social media to advertise and promote his talent.

He concluded, "After working hard to build this career, I refuse to work in an establishment where management allows unlicensed personnel. In this industry, we call them haircutters. Unruly or disrespectful clients are dealt with in a professional manner, and if the behavior persists, we all refuse to service that client." (See a sample of Ian's haircut at figure 13.13 below.)

Aaron Pulliam was one of the pioneers in bringing African American barbering to the Murrieta/Temecula area (personal interview, December 30, 2014). He said he has been in the industry for more than eighteen years.

His initial profession was truck driving, and he became disenchanted with it because he was on the road and away from his boys. His wife mentioned that she thought he did a sufficient job cutting his boys' hair, and she suggested he try the barbering field. Aaron said that after he completed barber school, he opened and operated a shop for almost fifteen years. After selling his shop, he pondered leaving the area, but decided to join Team Rico's barbering staff. He said,

> At Rico's, there is competition among the younger barbers, but not me, because I am comfortable with my abilities within the profession. I do not attend hair shows, because I am not into the designs. Although one may be able to pick up different techniques of servicing hair, the techniques I use have been working very well for me.
>
> A typical workweek for me is pretty exhausting, but the financial aspect is well worth it. The most challenging part of this job as an independent contractor is not having a retirement plan in place, and during nonpeak periods we sometimes sit and wait for a client to come, or a walk-in. The most enjoyable part of this job is the fun you have with both the clients and coworkers. Team Rico barbers have a special bond that I have not witnessed at other shops. I enjoy teasing my coworkers about their professional football and college teams.

Aaron wondered aloud why people spend the time and money to enter the barbering profession and within a short period—without having an opportunity to succeed—they find themselves doing something else.

> I felt that I was a fit for the team after the first day. Perhaps those leaving are not dedicated to the field, find barbering to be more challenging than anticipated, or lack the passion that is required to excel and sustain the financial lifestyle one desires.
>
> The barbering field is still dominated by males; however, there are more women now in the field than ever before. The ladies on Rico's staff can hold their own and have

> a clientele base to prove it. Coming to Rico's has been a blessing. I adjusted to the culture without a problem, and the atmosphere is great.
>
> Had I known earlier that there was no retirement plan for this industry, perhaps I would have changed my career path. I believe there should be a mandatory policy requiring barbers to put away so much monthly toward their own retirement plan. Maybe a plan could be established through management or the shop owner. Without a retirement plan, barbers are going to be in for a rude awakening when they get older and can no longer stand behind the chair.
>
> The most rewarding thing about my job is being able to talk smack about the San Diego Chargers. The laughter and fun at Rico's is exciting; the relationship is like a brotherhood.

Aaron said he is not a proponent of social media. And he would not work in a shop with an unlicensed person, because there are financial ramifications he would have to deal with if an inspector from the Board of Barbering and Cosmetology stopped by. In addition, the owner could lose the establishment license.

Aaron concluded, "There are temperamental clients in every service-oriented business. However, if an unruly, filthy-mouthed client does not respect the shop or me, I will communicate with them in a professional manner to stop or get their hair serviced someplace else."

Cicely Taddi has been cutting hair for two years (personal interview, December 31, 2014). She said, "I became a barber because I am a single mom and wanted a change from my career as a bartender. I was inspired to become a barber by a client that visited the bar I was working at. Another female barber and I started the barbering apprenticeship while

I was working as a bartender. Once I started in the barbershop, I fell in love with the craft and later learned I had the passion for this career path. My friend didn't have the passion, so she left the field altogether."

Cicely said that there is always competition among the barbers. "Our competition pushes each other, keeps you on your toes, and forces you to step your game up and get better. Rico's barbers desire every haircut that leaves the shop to be perfect. Otherwise, management may have to intervene. There are twelve barbers in the shop where I work, and there is minor workmanship from all of the barbers as it related to traditional haircuts."

Cicely said she attends hair shows because it provides her exposure to other barbers, inspiration, and different techniques, while encouraging camaraderie among the barbers. On a typically workweek for her, "Tuesday through Saturday is exhausting but financially rewarding. The part of my job I find most challenging is the discipline and acknowledging the fact that this is my own business. I am responsible for the amount of money I make. I love being my own boss and the freedom to know that I am in control is very enjoyable."

Cicely said that a lot of people leave the field because it is viewed as a hustle.

You must have people skills whereby you can communicate about world news, politics, and most definitely sports. If you lack in either of those areas, barbering is not the field for you. Barbering is still considered a male-dominated field. However, when I attend hair shows, I am seeing many more females in the industry. That is inspiring, and I hope I am in a position someday to recommend or inspire some other females to enter the field.

I adjusted to Team Rico's culture very easily. I feel like I'm at home." If the opportunity presented itself again for Cicely to change her career path, she said she would remain in the barbering field. "Once Team Rico's saw that I was serious about this barbering and the passion

I displayed, I felt accepted as a genuine fit. Real barbers take their craft serious, and once they feel your passion, you are all in. The most rewarding thing about my job is seeing a client's smile after I have put a nice, clean haircut on him. As a new female in the shop, clients are apprehensive to sit in my chair until they see my work."

Cicely added, "I am a proponent for the usage of social networks to advertise. Participation has paid off for me financially. If I found out that someone in a shop was unlicensed, I would approach management and make an effort to encourage the individual to get licensed."

According to her, clients in the barbershop are almost the same as in the bar. "I get flirted with often but have learned over the years how to keep the conversation professional. I am all about the pay for the hair services. However, if unruly clients persist, I ask them to stop or sit in someone else's chair. If they are really rude, there are plenty of men in the shop that will deal with them. (See a sample of Cicely's work at figure 13.14 below.)

Kendra Ricks has been doing hair and braiding since she was fourteen and is currently a licensed cosmetologist in the state of Maryland (personal interview, June 10, 2015). She recently relocated to California and lacks sufficient time for the reciprocity process. Kendra said she was inspired to enter the barbering apprenticeship program because she has a desire to learn all the facets of the hair-care industry.

Kendra has attended hair shows for women in Maryland but none for barbers. She feels that hair shows are an important component in helping the uninformed become more knowledgeable about the various new styles, try out new equipment, and gain product knowledge. Since she has been in the apprenticeship program, fading has become the most challenging part of haircuts for Kendra.

"The most enjoyable thing about working in the barbering field at Rico's is the camaraderie with the other practitioners," she said. "In addition, I feel a lot of cosmetologists are crossing over into the barbering field because it takes too much time to style female hair in comparison to what you can do in the barbering field."

Kendra said that barbering is still a male-dominated industry, but women are slowly but surely transitioning in. She added,

> Personally, I had no problem adjusting to the culture, because I knew immediately the staff accepted me with open arms and unconditionally. Although I was assigned two trainers to help me learn the various styles and techniques, all the other barbers chimed in and provided that much-needed constructive criticism. And I accept any and all feedback because I want to get better. I am not one to have thin skin. You really can't in this industry

Kendra said she loves the industry and wouldn't want to do anything else for a livelihood. She is a proponent of marketing yourself and products using social media; it has been profitable for her since arriving in the Shaky State (California).

"I am blessed to be able to work in my first shop with a wonderful diverse workforce," she said. "We are all like a family. I am rapidly learning what the different clippers work best for; that is the most confusing part for me."

Jordan Shipley was born and raised in San Diego, attended college at Lincoln University, and then worked a few warehouse jobs (personal interview, June 10, 2015). "However," he said, "[Barbering] is and has been the most enjoyable and rewarding job I've had since becoming an adult." After relocating to the Inland Empire, he enrolled at Mt. San Jacinto Community College. "A light finally came on in my memory. When I was young, my mother used to cut my hair, and she did a pretty good job. So that is where I got my inspiration to become a barber."

Jordan entered the barbering apprenticeship program on January 29, 2015. He said,

> Since joining the program, I realize the easiest part of being a barber is you are your own boss; it is your business, and you can make it what you want it to be. However, on the flip side of the coin, the most difficult part of being a barber for me is cutting long blond and red hair. Because of the nature of the color, it is difficult to blend [layer] properly. It is so rewarding to watch young kids get out of the chair and have a huge smile on their face as they view their hair makeover.

Jordan said he loves all aspects of being a barber. He learns a little from every barber in the shop, including other apprentices. He said, "If you get to the point where you can't learn from others, you're in the wrong business. The hair-care business is always evolving. As such, the hot towel shave has been eluding me, and I truly have a desire to master that aspect of the craft."

Jordan further noted that he came into the industry like many others—by being a professional haircutter. I asked him to differentiate between a haircutter and a barber. He said with a huge smile that a barber is licensed and regulated by the state, and a haircutter has no license, is unregulated, works from home or garage, and lacks the sanitation and hygiene that a barber possesses. Jordan said his coworkers immediately embraced him, and when they started complimenting him on his work, he realizes he was a fit and as truly accepted.

CHAPTER FOURTEEN

CLIENT'S PERSPECTIVE

During a personal interview with a Rico's client named Jerry, he told me he retired from Union Carbide (now Dow Chemical Company) as a sales and marketing person (personal interview, July 2, 2014). His job required traveling to various cities in Ohio, Texas, and Kansas. During many of his trips, out of necessity, Jerry sought out a place where African Americans could get their hair cut. Often the place he found was unsanitary and appeared to be unorganized.

When he moved to southern Riverside County, once again he needed to find a place for his hair-care services. A friend recommended Rico's #1. Jerry said,

> During my first visit to Rico's, I noticed several things about the shop: First and foremost, the cleanliness and arrangement of the shop truly impressed me; secondly, all of the barbers greeted me with a sense of warmth and sincerity; and thirdly, even as a walk-in I was permitted to choose the barber of my liking. I was so impressed with the service I received, I made the young man my primary barber. As such, I was able to make appointments for future service.

Jerry contended that appointments were unheard of in the shops he had utilized in the past. He also said that he could easily see that Rico's was organized and well managed, based on the courtesy of the staff and the longevity of the establishment.

Manny Pena has been a client of Rico's #1 for almost three years (personal interview, August 16, 2014). A friend referred him to Rico's, and since his primary barber relocated, he chose Jenny as his new primary barber. Prior to becoming a regular customer at Rico's, Manny was getting his hair-care services in San Diego.

On a scale of one to ten, Manny rated both as a ten. He said, "I'm not saying this because you are the owner; it is the best overall barbershop I've been in." He said he enjoys coming to Rico's because he can call and get an appointment. "It definitively takes the frustration out of having to wait an extended period to be serviced," he said. "If my barber has plans or an emergency and anticipates not working for an extended period of time, I would expect her to contact me and recommend a replacement barber in the same shop until she returns."

He continued, "The Internet makes it easy to communicate one's intentions with a mass of people without contacting them individually. My barber's dress is always appropriate, professional, and casual. I have and will continue to recommend others to my barber."

According to Manny, Rico's entertainment is top-notch, with televisions strategically located for all to view, music from excellent speakers—not loud or over-the-top—and free Wi-Fi access. The shop is lively, the staff is somewhat young, and the conversation is appropriate for a family. "However," Manny said, "I am a nonsmoker, and if my barber had a smoking smell emanating from his clothing, I would say something. If it persisted, I would find myself another barber."

Manny said, "Rico's prices are commensurate with the outstanding service they provide. I am a believer that you get what you pay for. I always get a good haircut and conversation."

Brian Goudeau said he has been a regular client of Rico's for three years, and his primary barber is Ian Fleming (personal communication, August 16, 2014). When he can't get in with Ian, he goes to another Rico's barber at either location. "Over the years, I've watch them all cut and grow professional," Brian said. "Therefore, I feel comfortable with that decision."

Brian said friend that he works with recommended Rico's. He has been totally satisfied with both Rico's and its staff. He said he prefers the appointment system because it provides him the flexibility of controlling his time. He further stated that he has no objections to the appearance of any of the staff and has recommended Rico's to others. "Rico's has a diverse staff," Brian said. "And I would have no objections to a Rico's female team member servicing my hair."

He added, "The content of the television and music both are tasteful and pleasing to view and listen. The [smell] of smoke emanating from one's clothing is a nonissue with me, and I would continue as a client." He also was pleased with the prices charged for hair-care services at Rico's.

Martel Pleasant has coming to Rico's about four years; he jumped around from barber to barber and settled for Cleve as his primary (personal interview, August 16, 2014). He said, "I was getting my hair cut in Moreno Valley, and I happen to meet Mr. Washington," he said. "He gave me a card and invited me to visit his shop with no recommendation as to what barber to see." He said he is absolutely satisfied with both his barber and Rico's because he is able to get weekly appointments and doesn't waste an inordinate amount of time. If or when Cleve is not available, Martel says he will just utilize one of the other barbers. He is satisfied with the professional competence they have shown.

"Cleve is a young man that dresses in a manner conducive to his work," Martel said. "I have and will continue to recommend others to Cleve.

Rico's has proven its diversity in both staff and clients. I will have no problem allowing a female to service my hair."

Martel added, "I am gratifying to see a barbershop with various entertainments for clients in the form of multi-channel television, Internet music, and Wi-Fi accessibility. The prices are very reasonable too."

In a personal interview (August 16, 2014), Lionel Brown said he had been a loyal client of Rico's for the better part of seven years, and his barber is Nick. Lionel was born and raised in Long Beach and was utilizing a barber in Carson, a town adjacent to where he was raised, until he found out about the talent at Rico's. He said he learned about Rico's while shopping at a local food chain; he noticed a brother with a good-looking haircut and asked who cut his hair. The man gave him a business card for one of Rico's barber. "When it came time for my next cut," Lionel said, "I came to Rico's, and the rest is history. On a scale of one to ten, he gave both Rico's and his barber a ten because he is overwhelmingly pleased with both.

Lionel said that appointments are best suited for him because of his schedule. He can't afford to sit for hours to get a haircut because of the daily volume of clients who enter. "If Nick ever becomes inaccessible to me for a haircut, I won't panic, because of the versatility and professional competence of Team Rico." He had no problems with the way Nick dressed or his overall appearance and said he would continue to highly recommend others to him. Lionel also said he would not hesitate to allow a Rico's female barber to cut his hair.

Lionel added, "Rico's entertainment is hilarious at times, and the shop always has good energy. If a barber smelled of smoke, I wouldn't say anything to him about it, as long as he conducts himself professionally. And I have no problem with the prices I pay for hair-care services."

Lucas A. Cotto said he has been coming to Rico's a little over two years, and Big Jack is his barber. "I was stationed in Hawaii prior to moving to Murrieta. I went to several barbershops and was not satisfied. I found out about Rico's from my wife. She drove by the shop, and I went in. Since then, it has been the barbershop for my son and me. I am totally satisfied with both my barber and Rico's."

Like the majority of Rico's clients, Lucas prefers an appointment over walking in because as a family man he does not have the time to waste an hour or two hoping to get a cut and back to his routine. "If Big Jack is not available to cut my hair, I have no problem going to Cleve," he said. "He too is a very talented young barber who displays outstanding professional savvy for his experience."

Lucas said that the appearance of all of Rico's barbers is excellent for the service they provide. "I have and will continue to recommend others to the shop." He also said he has no apprehensiveness about letting a female cut his or his son's hair. Additionally, he felt Rico's entertainment is superb because all the televisions have an individual cable box; when there are kids in the shop, a television station can be dedicated to them. The music is always played at a moderate tone and pleasing to the ear. He added, Rico's is the first barbershop I've been in with available and published Wi-Fi accessibility.

If a barber had the smell of smoke radiating from his or her clothing, I would not say anything; however, if it was alcohol, I would mention it to the barber and management. If that became continuous, I would get another barber.

The energy at Rico's is phenomenal. Every time I come in I am properly greeted. They always have a story to tell you in a good atmosphere, good times, and a great place to take your family. My conversation with Big Jack is always about family. Cleve is always entertaining.

My youngest son just went to Jenny for the first time, and he is somewhat of an introvert when it comes to strangers. However, Jenny was able to get him to relax, and they had a full-blown conversation while he was getting his hair cut.

CHAPTER FIFTEEN

INDUSTRY KILLERS

As with most regulated and legitimate industries, problems exist in barbering and are brought about by those who want to be in the industry legally but cannot for various reasons. These parasites find ways to infiltrate the hair-care industry by parading as legitimate barbers. These are unskilled butchers who use unsanitary equipment, in an effort to make a quick dollar, are nothing more than haircutters.

Who can we blame for this? First and foremost, it is the establishment owners' responsibility to allow these people in their shops only as customers. Second, it is a licensed barber's responsibility to refuse to work with unlicensed personnel. Doing so forces establishment owners to do the right thing and hire skilled, licensed practitioners.

And yes, there are some bad establishment owners in the industry who allow both licensed barbers and haircutters to dress any way they'd like. One may enter a barbershop and find workers in shorts, open-toe shoes, or flip-flops, with pants hanging down by their rectum, crazy music blasting loud enough to be heard for blocks, and garbage spewing from their mouths, so filthy it should be flushed down the toilet.

Owners must also contend with drug- and alcohol-related issues. Barbers in certain geographic areas have come to the conclusion that they can get high on a foreign substance or alcohol and return to work without it being noticed. I am not advocating full abstinence but abstinence during working hours.

Then there are some barbers that feel they are too good or experienced to cut small children's hair. Get real! Small children will be around longer as your clients than most of your older clients. You must consider dollars in conjunction with common sense.

Shop owners; please stop making your waiting clients sit in your shop without having the creature comforts necessary to sustain them. When it's hot, turn on the air-conditioner, and turn on the heat when it's cold.

Barbershops that advertise their operating hours on the window should ensure they have someone there for the duration.

If you enter a shop and the floor is filthy and no one is getting a haircut, more than likely the equipment that will be used on you will be filthy as well.

Customers have the right to ask to view the license of anyone providing a hair-care service, and I strongly recommend that you do so. If they can't produce a current valid license for your state, you should not allow them to service you.

Practitioners, please use appropriate language that is pleasing to the ear. You also must understand that if you make an appointment for someone, you must honor it. As customers, you have a responsibility to be on time for that appointment or to notify the barber about your tardiness and provide an estimate of when you can arrive. Barbers are not obligated to keep a chair vacant. An appointment in this industry means you are the next one up after the person currently in the chair. Time is money and money is time; they complement each other.

Barbers, get those darn cellphone earplugs out of your ears while servicing a client. Your client is paying you for 100 percent of your attention. How can you give it if you are on the phone with your honey?

It is also impolite to communicate with clients or prospective clients while you are seated. Get off your rear end, look them in the eye, and communicate effectively.

Female barbers, please stop trying to fit in with the guys; just be yourself, and you will be accepted. The men will have no choice if you let your clippers and razors do your talking. Remember, barbershops are still and always will be male oriented. Do expect to hear venom spewed by both barbers and clients alike. Don't complain when you are hit on; in your own way, deal with it in a respectable manner. Your male counterparts will always have your back.

CHAPTER SIXTEEN

EFFECTIVE COMMUNICATION

It is crucial that establishment owners create a winning culture within their organizations. The atmosphere must be conducive to both the workers and the customers. Effective communication provides clear guidelines and expectations for both barbers and the clientele they serve. Established expectations also help the barbers understand how they present themselves both inside and outside the establishment will impact the business.

Effective communication also lets the barber know what is required to achieve positive feedback. Constructive criticism may not always be accepted. The key is the delivery. Only by demonstrating empathy and working together to resolve a situation can people accomplish their personal and professional goals. A good barber knows when to talk, while a great barber knows when to listen. Which one are you?

According to Rosenberg (2003), observing without evaluating is the highest form of human intelligence. You must be an attentive and focused listener prior to attempting to assess what was actually transmitted verbally. However, there could be a heavy price to pay if your true feelings are not expressed. You must never make another feel that what he or she voiced was less important than what others had to say. Communications with clientele must always be positive. Being positive allows the barber to manage what is expected from the client regarding the hair-care service he or she desires.

Organizational loyalty and trust can be achieved only through effective communication. They are the foundation for humanizing and enhancing strong relationships with clients while establishing solid marketing about your hair-care services, retail products, and organizational culture.

As the leader of your establishment, it is essential that you keep lines of communication open. Doing so could lead to new ideas and innovations in areas that could be beneficial to the entire organization. Most barbers know what is important to the survivability of the barbershop they work in and frequently have good ideas for making improvements; they also know of opportunities that can improve marketability.

Sometimes the main obstacle is getting someone to pay attention. Therefore, barbershop and salon owners who employ barbers must be open-minded and receptive to new ideas. Once this is noticed, other practitioners will be more likely bring forth their ideas. Customers can also be used to ascertain ideas to improve hair-care services. Customer ambassadors are the easiest way to obtain free marketing and advertising. But if the service is bad, ambassadors can destroy your business.

Effective organizational communication is the foundation for cultivating strong teamwork among your hair-care workforce, with everyone working together to achieve one common goal. Shop owners must provide practitioners with knowledge and provide the structured, safe, and positive work environment they need to feel comfortable if a conflict arises. They also need to know how it will be resolved. Hunter (2005) says that only by demonstrating empathy and working together to resolve a situation can both the professional and the personal goals be accomplished. Often, educated leaders communicate to an audience rather than the people. The common man does not want to listen to a lot of intellectual words that require a dictionary to understand. People in general just want to be heard and not have their voices blocked as if they are not meaningful.

Summary

Modern Barbers and Barbering

Barbering in America began with barber-surgeons. As with any industry, there were customs and traditions.

Barbers continued the practices of bloodletting, minor surgery, using herbal remedies, and tooth pulling for centuries. These barber-surgeons formed their first organization in France in 1096 and by the 1100s had formed guilds of surgeons that specialized in the study of medicine.

In 1893, A. B. Moler established America's first barber school in Chicago. In that same year, he published the first barbering textbook, *The Moler Manual of Barbering.* Minnesota was the first state to pass a barber-licensing law. This legislation was passed in 1897, setting the standards for sanitation, minimum education, and licensing requirements for barbers and barbershops in that state.

Regulating the Hair-Care Industry

Since 1929, all states, with the exception of several counties in Alabama, had passed laws regulating the practice of barbering and hairstyling. In California, the Department of Consumer Affairs's Board of Barbering and Cosmetology is the governing body responsible for regulating the hair-care industry, including testing and licensing master barbers, cosmetologists, and barber apprentices. In addition, this governing body regulates the licensing of hair-care establishments. The board's primary responsibility is the protection of the health, safety, and welfare of the public as it relates to hair care (California Barbering, 2013).

The Transition of Barbershop Locations

Many who have been in the hair-care industry for an extended period knows that there has been and continues to be a rapid decline in number of the traditional neighborhood barbershops. Some suggest that the cause could be the increasing number of national chain-operated hair-care establishments operating in close proximity to neighborhoods. Some suggest that the neighborhood barbershops had to relocate to malls or strip malls to stay in business and to remain competitive.

Client and Workforce Diversity

In general, many barbershops and hair salons, both privately owned and retail chain establishments, catered to one race and one gender, and their workforce were basically the same. A survey conducted during the dissertation process revealed that 95 percent of the shop owners surveyed did not support a diverse workforce, even if the clientele base was diverse.

Artistic Styling

At the turn of the twentieth century, men's hairstyles included chemicals, braids, crew cuts, pompadours, flat tops, afros, and the like. That fad was short-lived as women started wearing short hair and getting haircuts at what were once traditional male barbershops. More recently, young barbers became innovative and artistic, cutting letters and designs into haircuts or styles. These young artists challenged their abilities by attending or competing in various hair shows. Facebook, Instagram, texting, and other means of communication have been used to promote these pioneers as they have taken barbering to the next level.

Barbershop Entertainment

During the sixties in the South, the music was mostly soft jazz, blues, or Gospel. Since the advent of the Internet, the capabilities exist to connect with music stations around the world and to download music. Generation Y practitioners have taken full advantage of the situation. The entertainment in many barbershops has transitioned to the desires of the barbers. The music in hair-care establishments now tends to be loud, boisterous rap music with lyrics that seasoned clients can't understand.

Professional Image

It is important for barbers to keep both their head and their facial hair looking healthy and clean. Your hair should always be up to date. Barbers are selling haircuts and overall appearance, and appearance can make all the difference when seeking to gain and keep a new client. A barber's clothes should be clean, freshly ironed, and stain-free. Even if you have a uniform or mandatory dress code, you still have some control over how you look. Your clothes should fit properly—not too tight, baggy, or sagging, with no undergarments showing. Female barbers should refrain from wearing a skirt, dress, or blouse with spaghetti straps. Customers' notice when you take pride in your appearance. Females, if you have the freedom to wear whatever you want, be careful not to send the wrong signal. You are in the barber profession, and you should make sure you look like a professional. The more professional you look, the more your clients will have confidence in your ability.

Industry Etiquette

The barbershop is a black man's country club. Your barber is not just a barber; he or she is a friend, confidante, psychologist, oracle, telepathist, or anything else you need for that day. The barber is a creator of the look a man presents to the world. For any special event, preparation starts with a haircut. The barbershop is a microcosm of the black community, and it is a place where you can be yourself and where truth is always expected. No barber wants to deal with a customer who demeans, disrespects, or treats him or her as a subordinate. The goal for both should be a long-lasting, healthy relationship.

Camaraderie and Morale

Matching a barber with your organizational culture is critical to a proper fit. A person who is a good fit for your barbershop culture will transition easily and be a valuable asset. A barbering staff requires inclusiveness through diversity while having similar backgrounds and interests. Any misalignment of organizational culture will affect the morale and camaraderie of the staff. Establishment owners must be careful not to align cultural fit with discrimination. Keep in mind that Webster's defines camaraderie as mutual trust and friendship among people who spend a lot of time together.

Mentorship

A mentorship program allows a barber apprentice to learn while at the same time ear a living. All work is accomplished under the direct supervision of a master barber. Your mentor will be able to explain the inner-workings on how to perfect the craft and prepare you for the ultimate, the state written and practical examinations.

Social Responsibility

Barbershops should have in place a viable and consistent corporate social-responsibility program. Establishment owners should take the lead and solicit participation. Barbers get to meet new people, so they should become part of that community. A good place to start is with community school athletic programs or shelters for battered women. Clients are the lifeblood of any organization.

An Establishment Owner's Perspective

John Olivas has been in the hair-care industry for more than fifty years, as barber, cosmetologist, barber school owner, barber/cosmetologist instructor, and barber supply store operator. He believes the best days for traditional barbering have passed. According to John, the new barbers are entering the field to make a quick buck and live the fast life. They lack passion and dedication to the field. You can see it in the way they dress and communicate in the presence of women and children.

Practitioners' Perspectives

All barber practitioners in my study were asked the same questions, and they all entered the field initially because of financial reasons. But it became a passion to them. They also noted that there is competition among coworker to push each other to be the best barbers they can be.

Barbers said that hair shows are attended primarily to pick up on the latest trends, techniques, and tools that are being used in the industry. They further suggested that those anticipating entering the field be prepared for a physically demanding workweek that could pan out to be financially rewarding. They concluded by saying the barbering field is still male dominated, but women are beginning to make their mark in the industry.

Clients' Perspectives

The clients surveyed were asked the same questions, and they revealed the following:

- They heard about Rico's by looking at someone's haircut and asking who did, or purely by word of mouth.
- They were satisfied with their barber.
- They were pleased with the culture and atmosphere of Rico's.
- Appointments were preferable to walking in.
- If their barber was unavailable, they would use another barber.
- They recommended their barber to others.
- The women working at Rico's could cut hair just as skillfully as their male counterpart.

Industry Killers

Establishment owners must foster the blame for some of the negative detractors within the hair care industry. Many of the things that hurt the hair care industry were mentioned in Chapter Fifteen of this book. However, there may be others, but the industry must police itself otherwise the negative connotation that surrounds it will become even greater. If that remains the case clients will seek their hair care needs from nationwide franchise shops that operates under strict professional guidelines.

Effective Communication

It is crucial that establishment owners create a winning culture within their organizations. The atmosphere must be conducive to both the workers and the customers. Only by demonstrating empathy and working together to resolve issues can people accomplish their personal and professional goals (Hunter, 2005). A good barber knows when to talk, while a great barber knows when to listen. Which one are you?

REFERENCES

Alexander, D. n.d. "How to Talk to Your Barber or Stylist: Talk your way into a great haircut." http://menshair.about.com/od/yoursalonvisit/a/How-To-Talk-To-Your-Barber-Or-Stylist.htm

"Barbershop and Salon Etiquette: Barber and stylist pet peeves to avoid. http://menshair.about.com/od/yoursalonvisit/a/Barbershop-And-Salon-Etiquette.htm

Bock, W. 2005. "Supervisory Leadership: Leadership is an apprenticeship trade." http://www.agreatsupervisor.com/articles/apprenticetrade.htm#top.

California Barbering and Cosmetology Act and Regulation. 2013. Business & Professions Code, Division 3, Chapter 10. Retrieved from http://barbercosmo.ca.gov/.

California Department of Industrial Relations, Division of Apprenticeship Standards. n.d. Retrieved from http://www.dir.ca.gov/divisions_and_programs.html.

Green, M. 2014. "The Barber is Back," *Oregon Business Magazine*, June 3, 2014, 37, 5.

Hunter, S. 2005. "Creating a Winning Atmosphere in Your Company." Retrieved from http://agreatsupervisor.com/articles/huntercreatewinning.htm.

Leland, J. 2009. "The Art of Manliness: How to Pick a Barber." http://www.artofmanliness.com/2009/08/18/how-to-pick-a-barber/.

Levin, A. 2011. "Some Barbershops Aren't Just for Haircuts Anymore." *Psychiatric News*, July 15, 2011, 46, 14.

Man Code. 2012. "The Barbershop: A black man's country club." http://mancodelaw. blogspot.com/2012/05/barbershop-black-mans-country-club.html

Releford, B. J., et al. 2010. "Cardiovascular Disease Control Through Barbershops: Design of a Nationwide Outreach Program." National Medical Association, 102.4, 336, 45.

Scali-Sheahan, Maura. 2011. Milady's Standard Professional Barbering. Clifton Park, NY: Milady.

Shelly-Maloney Apprentice Labor Standards Act of 1939. as amended, Chapter 4 of Division 3, Labor Code of the State of California.)

Small Business Encyclopedia: Social Responsibility. n.d. http://www.entrepreneur. com/encyclopedia/social-responsibility

Rosenberg, M. B. 2003. Nonviolent *Communications: A language of life.* Encinitas, CA:

Puddle Dancer Press.

"Survey Results: How Men Choose their Barbers and Stylists." August 3, 2011. https://www.swipely.com/blog/survey-results-how-men-choose-their-barbers-and-stylists.htm

TABLES

Table 4.1

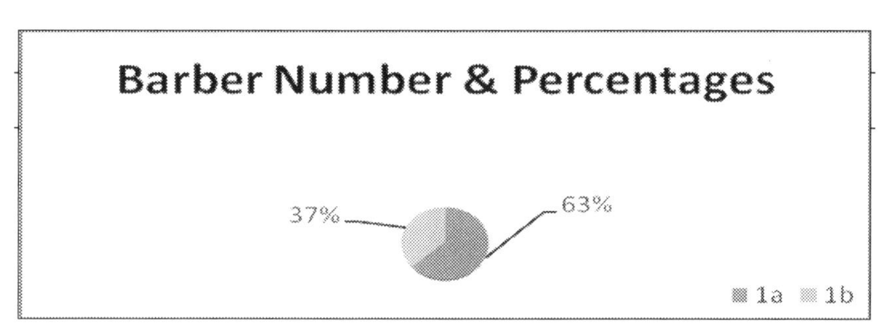

Table 4.2

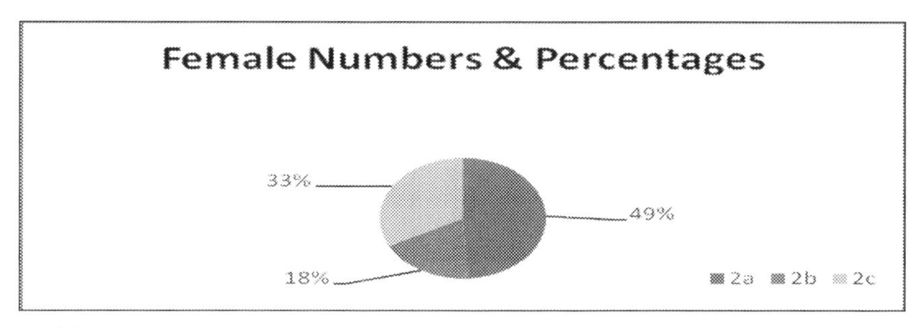

Table 4.3

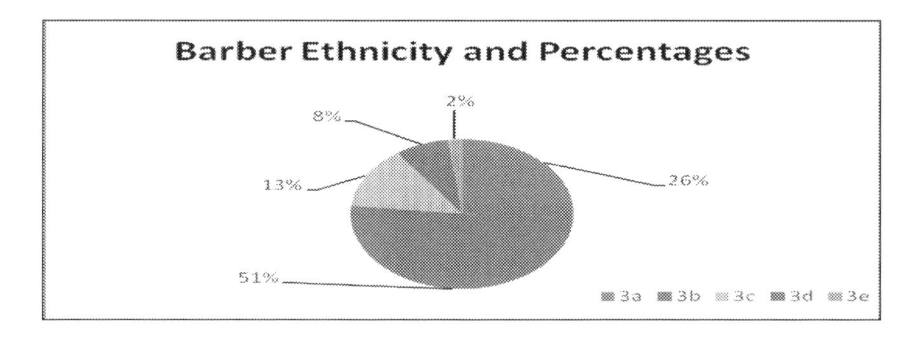

Table 4.4

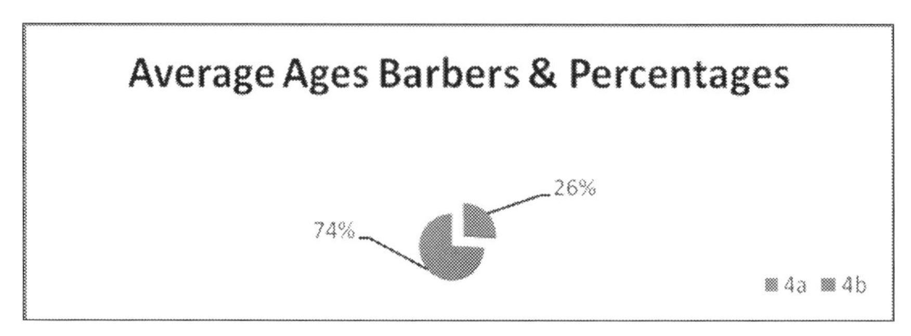

Table 4.5

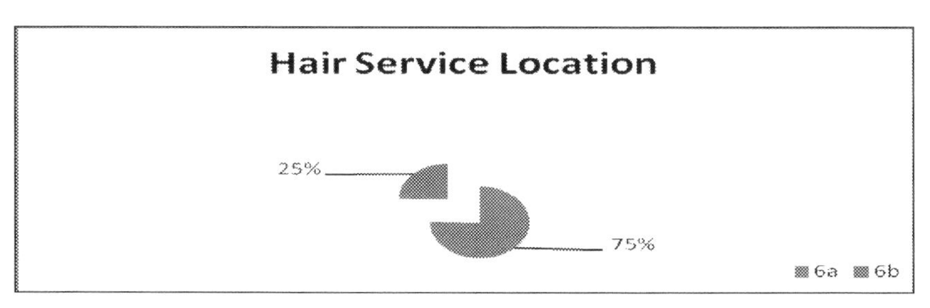

Table 4.6

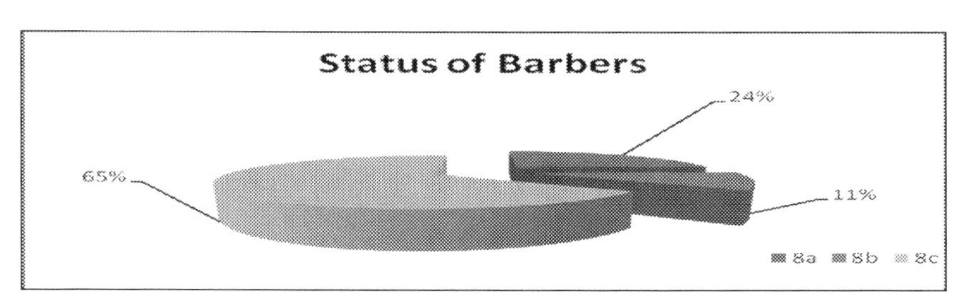

Table 4.7

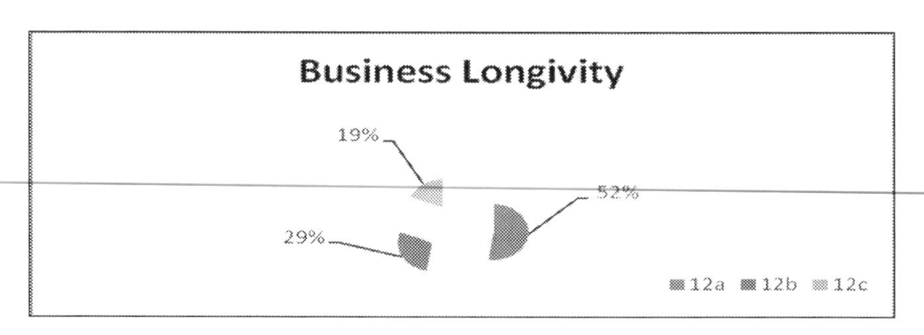

Table 4.8

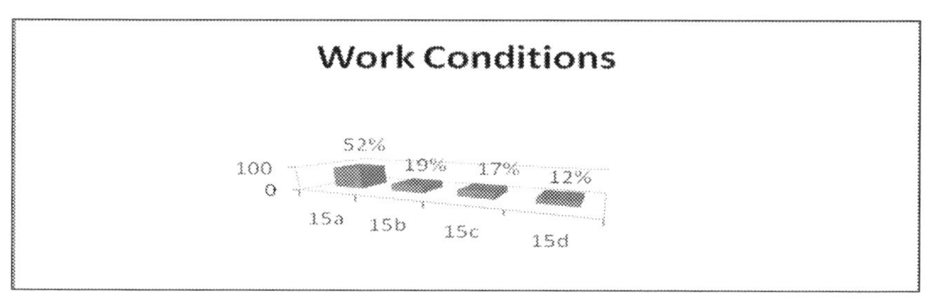

Table 4.9

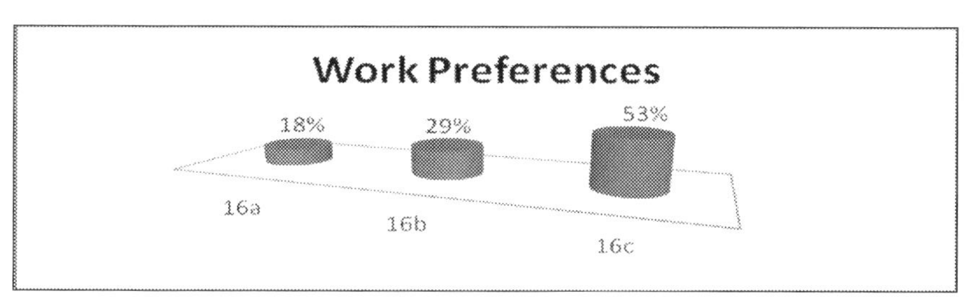

Table 4.10

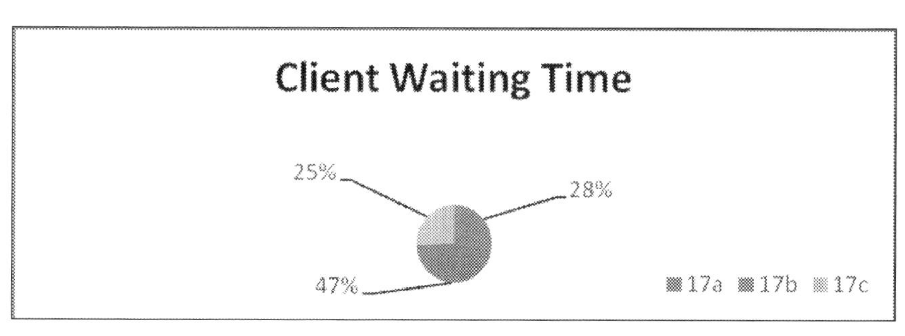

Table 4.11

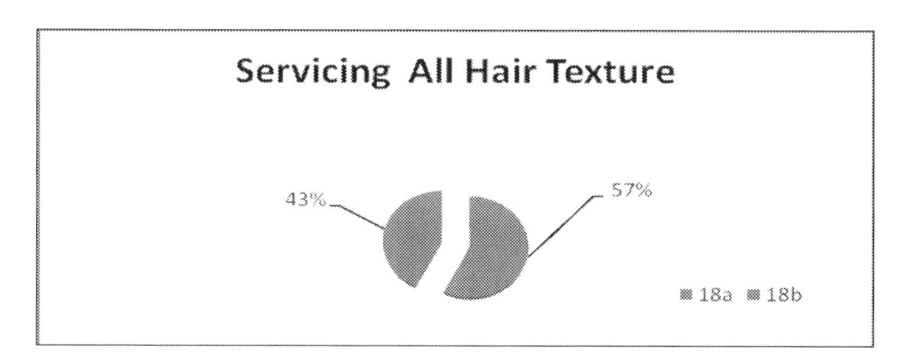

Table 4.12

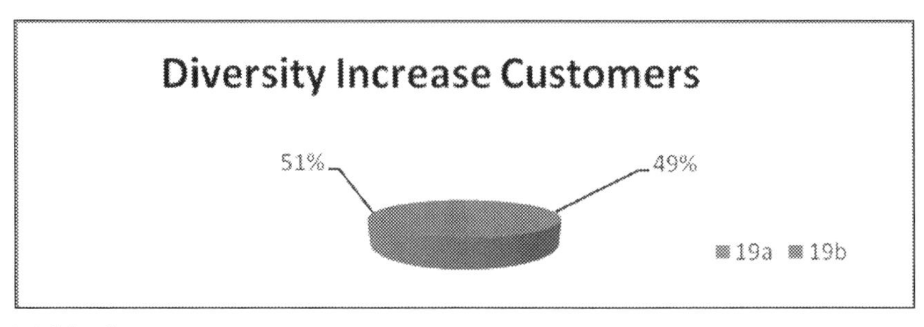

Table 4.13

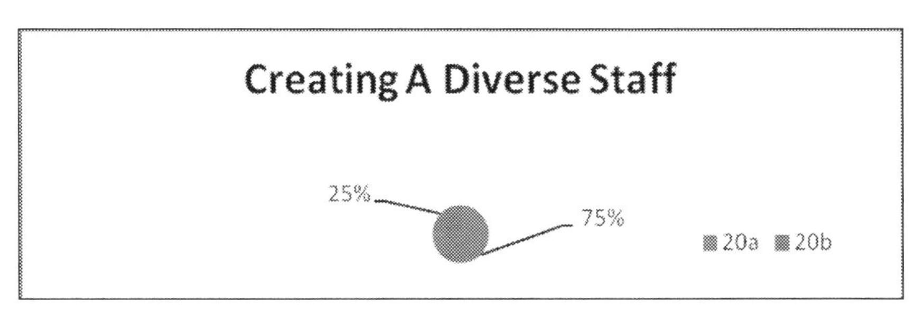

Table 4.14

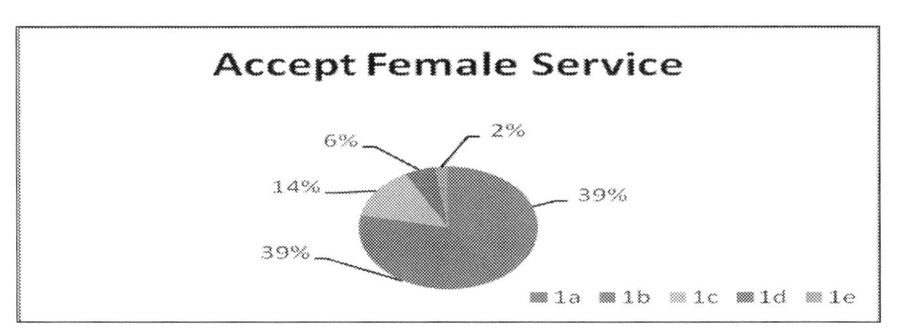

Table 4.15

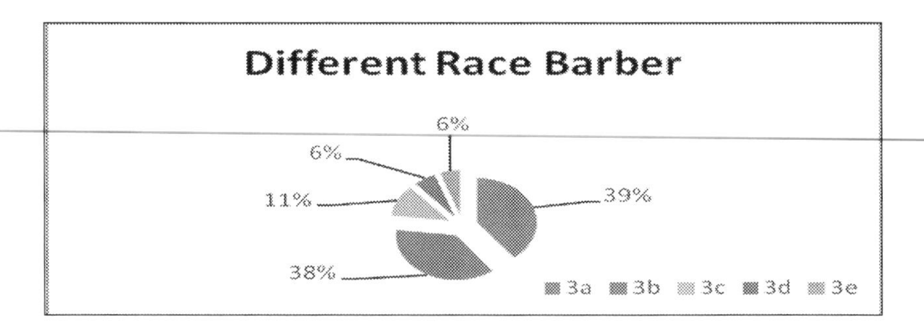

Table 4.16

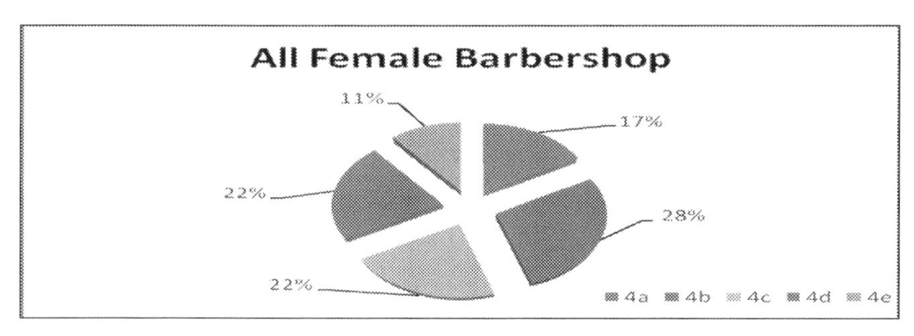

Table 4.17

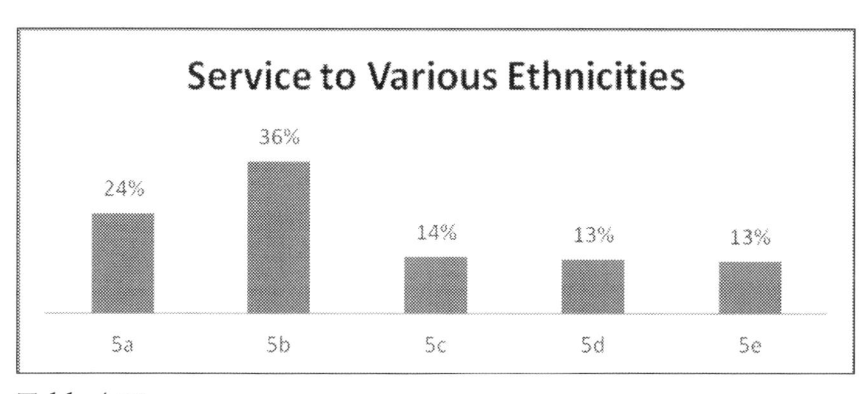

Table 4.18

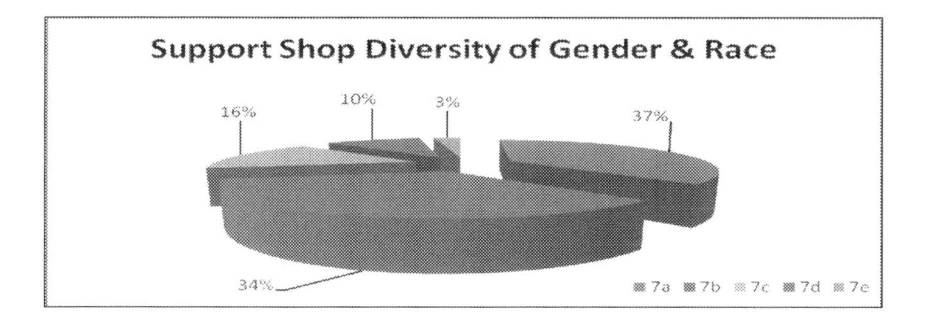

Table 4.19

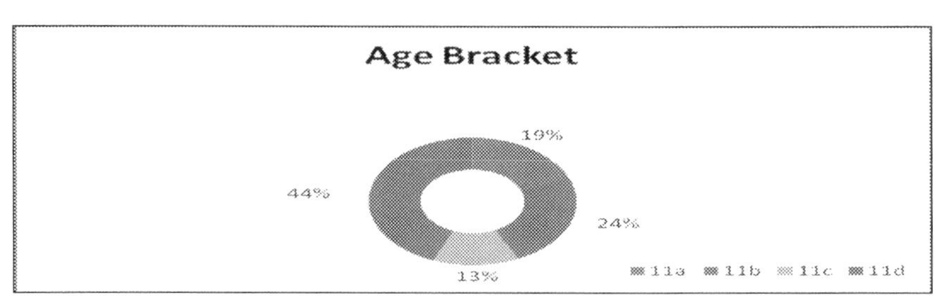

Table 4.20

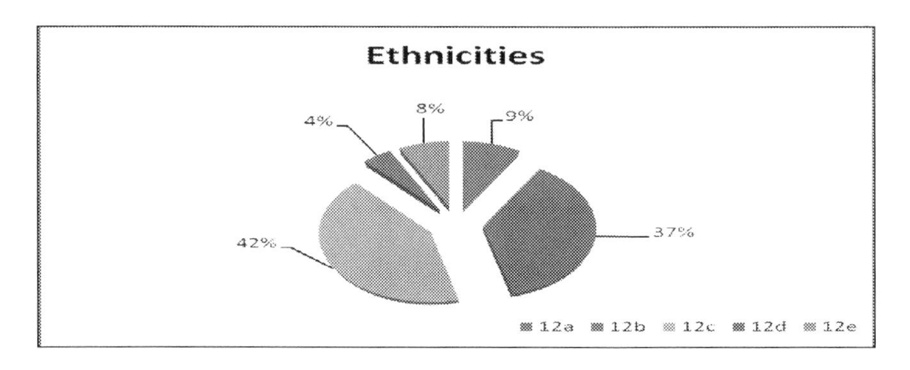

Rico's

Printed in the United States
By Bookmasters